The Best Deal

A trilogy

Rob Long

Chiselbury

The Best Deal

'Dogs have given us their absolute all. We are the centre of their universe. We are the focus of their love and faith and trust. They serve us in return for scraps.

It is without a doubt the best deal man has ever made.'

Roger Caras
President Emeritus ASPCA

'Gone to ground'
Parson Russell Terriers

For Gloria
and *all* our faithful friends.

With special thanks to
many unwitting hosts at home and in France.

Contents

Book Three ~ The Waif's Tail

Foreword

'…terriers are born with four times as much original sin in them as other dogs.'

Jerome K Jerome

Three men in a boat

France with Darcey, a brief and largely humorous daily diary, was written in 2007 during a carefree fun filled month mostly spent pottering around and about France's Mediterranean *départements.* Apart from topping and tailing the original journal, I never expected to add to it but inevitably, things change. Overtaken by events and since Jack Russell's terriers are clearly blessed with a surfeit of sinfulness, it seemed appropriate to embark on a sequel, *No Criticisms.* Because both narratives are not overly long and in the face of good advice willingly offered but woefully ignored, I amalgamated them. It seemed sensible. In editing the material I strived to preserve the individual nature of our stories.

There things lay until 2022 when, in the space of a few short months, our latest terrier companions, first Sam and then Elle, followed Darcey in succumbing to serious illnesses and sadly passed away. Not long afterwards Patch, an elderly Parson Russell Terrier, was discovered needing a home for the evening of his years and we adopted him.

As a result I began *The Waif's Tail,* a brief introduction and progress report, written to acknowledge his contribution to our welfare in the evening of *all* our years.

Whilst writing *The Waif's Tail* I revisited *France with Darcey* and *No Criticisms* and considered whether to amend or redact some of their more outdated and outrageous contents, after all, ideas, attitudes and technology have all moved on over the last fifteen years. In the end, remembering that 'The past is a foreign country; they do things differently there', I decided not to do so especially as I doubt anyone would see customers in a Perpignan cafe 'smoking and clearly enjoying it' these days!

Throughout our doggy adventures I attempted to keep matters light and entertaining. I also tried to avoid introducing introductions. It might be argued that I've done exactly that here.

Orchard House

2022

Amuse-bouche

A complementary bite sized tempter

Provence is cold in mid February. Even in the strong sunlight under cloud free skies bleached to shades of faded blue denim, temperatures struggle, and in the still of night, beneath a vast and glistening canopy of stars, the day's slight warmth drains rapidly and intense frosts are not uncommon.

The fair-weather denizens of this typically hot and dry landscape seize every opportunity to deplore the downright unfairness of inclement conditions. The Mistral; winter's ice and snow; the region's occasional lashing rainstorms, each and every ordeal a personal affront, are favourite and regular targets for their invective. During such disagreeable crises, *les Provençaux,* or at least a good proportion of them, are often to be observed, hunched dismally in favoured cafes and bars, sharing their misery with cronies; each grumbling and muttering into their morning coffee about the sheer injustice of dirty weather.

To be fair, the locals are largely resigned to winter with its lack of heat and holiday trade as there is a pause between acts whilst the country draws breath during a well earned intermission. Even so all is not idleness; everyday life continues apace. At the weekly open air markets the wrapped and muffled street traders stamp their feet against the biting cold and maintain a brisk, business as usual air. Although the markets lack summer's vigour and colour but certainly not the clamour, the cast of regulars buy and sell and deal, and urgent Must Not Be Missed offers and debatable bargains, still abound.

Elsewhere in the hushed ordered vineyards, early pruning is just starting - while in towns and villages the proprietors of shops and restaurants restock and sporadically maintain the set, taking the opportunity to carry out low season upkeep and repairs. Along the highways and byways summer's promise is evident as the very earliest of spring blossom splashes the verges with delicate arrangements of dramatic white, lit with subtle hints of pink. Everywhere the stage is being dressed and the players prepare to don costume before the arrival of summer's tourists.

Contrary to popular fiction the French are generous hosts and in the main they cope manfully with out of season guests and their fractured fifth-form attempts at the language of diplomacy. We are early visitors having arrived too soon for the show but in spite of that, are made welcome. We take a late lunch in the hills above the Rhône valley at Vaison la Romaine, where our cafe's sunny open terrace overlooks the spectacular gorge of the river L'Ouvéze spanned by its ancient Roman bridge. The original medieval village clings to the cliffs opposite, casting its shadows over the far bank where Vaison's war dead are ranked for eternity and the glory of France, and the church clock rings the hours.

At the cafe *Monsieur* is unusually brisk and utterly unperturbed by our tardiness. Recognising my Daily Telegraph he attempts *franglaise* whilst dealing the winning hand of menus.   *Madame* is solicitous and her simple lunch excellent.   Replete we pay a moderate bill and part friends. Whilst bidding us farewell, *Monsieur,* all over pompous with both national pride and foolish expectations, ventures that France will soundly beat the England Rugby Union XV at the Stade de France next weekend - I disabuse him!

As well as improving my rusty and painfully inadequate French, rashly airing such over-the-top patriotism is something I shall have to be carefully about when eventually we find a house and settle in France. Over time I have discovered that, however convivial the company, the penalties - usually hefty rounds of pastis for the equally jingoistic French fans - when the England team loses, as from time to time it surely must, are likely to be expensive.

For the sake of completeness and to rub just a little salt into the wounds, the English side beat France 24 to 13 away.

Book One

France with Darcey

Darcey Bussell

Our Jack Russell Terrier companion

Odyssey *(n.):*

An extended adventurous voyage or trip

An intellectual or spiritual quest

Diary *(n.):*

A daily record, especially a personal record of events

A book for use in keeping a personal record

Chapter One

Whys and wherefores

It's an odd thing for people of my generation but I managed to retire twice. After rewarding and often exciting, military service I endured brief and unplanned unemployment before embarking on a second career, no less stimulating, in business. Later on, early retirement, just sitting back and not having to work, turned out to be challenging; the army's description of boring. But, with time on our hands and just a few means in the bank, my wife and I have resolved to make up for lost time and missed opportunities.

Having soldiered here, there and not quite everywhere for some twenty-six years we were used to a nomadic lifestyle. In business, usually due to the demands of ambition's greasy pole, we continued the practice occasionally upping sticks and moving on whenever needs must. Enjoying short holidays in France and Spain as and when the opportunity arose was a welcome bonus as well as providing a powerful incentive to consider alternatives to retiring in England. The notion of changing our retirement strategy from Nesting to Investing and moving abroad became more compelling as time progressed.

A limiting factor was our dogs.

We've always been dog lovers and so over the years have been owned by a succession of rescued waifs and strays. It was my late father who introduced us to Jack Russell terriers. During the latter part of the 1970s he was a senior police officer stationed at Aldershot - Home of the British Army welcomes careful drivers. (*Since that's what its road signs proudly proclaim, we've always, tongue firmly in cheek, described it exactly that way.*) Family memory, fondly corroborated long after his death, has it that when on duty in that mid evening hiatus - somewhere between Opening Time and Last Orders, in an age when a semi-professional standard of snooker was high on the police agenda - the Old Man had taken to enjoying an evening pipe whilst strolling across the police station's yard. Commonly enough in those long lost, ever sunlit, pre-politically correct days, it seems that the county police maintained good order, solved the odd crime and housed stray dogs, whilst managing to find time for recreational pursuits, as well as indulging in tobacco and, no doubt, strong ale. Invariably his leisurely ramble took him through the strays' kennels just to inspect the runners and riders before a serious and demanding couple of frames.

During one such interlude he spotted among the town's current crop of lost and abandoned dogs a young female Jack Russell Terrier incarcerated for the mandatory seven days and scheduled by The Rules to be put down if by then unclaimed. Clearly this potential outrage to Dogdom could not be permitted and the old softy registered his name to rescue her should she remain masterless by the week's end.

So it transpired that a few days later, about eleven pm, father having completed his afternoon and early evening shift, my dear mother, by then comfortably abed, was the surprise recipient of an anonymous piebald squirm which arrived with an appetite the size of a Black Hole - accompanied by a side order of fleas. My father later told me that recognising her (*the dog of course!*) for the thoroughbred that she was, he was surprised by the lack

10

of any competition to re-home her and secretly delighted that her previous owners never bothered to seek her out.

Thus it was that Samantha, ever after known as Sammy, became the first of these charming working terriers to share our lives and grew to be a big influence on what was to follow. The outcome was never disagreeable and for all their occasional inconveniences, we've welcomed canine companions to the family whenever possible; *plus ca change, plus c'est la même*, mostly Jack Russell terriers.

Another consideration was the house.

After leaving the forces one of the good things about becoming an apprentice civilian was living full-time with my wife once more. On reflection I regret that, towards the tail end of my army career, I'd devoted far too much time to full blooded professional soldiering, only occasionally indulging in leaves of absence and sporadic bouts of weekend husbandry - 'Bean stealing' in the army's vocabulary and a choice I'd certainly not make again. Quite whether my wife would agree is another matter.

From time to time the demands of business obliged us to live in places neither of us much cared for. We have always valued the creature comforts and immediate neighbourhood of our latest 'nest' and the sheer delights of its surrounding moorlands but, (*there's always a 'but'*) we are rather less enamoured of the local towns and cities. Frankly, apart from the house's undoubted convenience and the wilds, we would have preferred to have settled somewhere else.

In retirement we were now in a position to vote with

our feet - we could sell up, resettle and together with our current companion, a rescued cross bred Jack Russell called Darcey, lotus-eat anywhere we chose.

Might a move to France be the answer?

Chapter Two

A Road Less Travelled

"Dear diary,

14th February At Home

We have always travelled light and based our packing on the inflexible rule that if it won't fit in one large grip and a suit fold it doesn't go.   In any case my wife is officer-in-charge packing and I find it prudent to remember that at all times.   Thus on the morning of departure it came as something of a surprise to discover the Saab's boot full of luggage and its back seat full of Darcey - scuppering at a stroke my, now somewhat rash, boast that we'd have the soft top down before Dijon. Our friends, charitably declining to take advantage of my immoderate bragging, waved us off cheerfully and even took photographs of the event; leading me to wonder if their offers to accommodate the dog while we were away had been entirely genuine."

But I am well ahead of myself...

Plotting and Planning.

In one of those inspired 'Oh let's just do it' moments we had decided to take to the road for an extended early spring reconnaissance of likely places in which to retire, and southern France headed our list. This brief, some might argue spare, journal, embroidered here and there with reminiscences - memories of and nostalgia for a moderately misplaced youth - is a mildly ironic account of our largely agreeable adventures at home and abroad.

🐕 🐕

The plans for our trip became viable once the vexed question of what to do with Darcey had been resolved.

For the sake of clarity, the dog Darcey is a Jack Russell Terrier who, while somewhat overlarge for the Kennel Club's breed standard, fully measures up to its more worthy requirements as she's a compact, courageous, rather independent character. She has been firmly established as the third member of the household for some fifteen years and since she was at least two, perhaps three (*possibly more, she having no way to tell us*) when liberated from a local dogs' home, she's attained respectable old age. This achievement, now unfortunately coupled with a tiresome heart condition, has failed to curb her lingering adolescence. Instead stiffened joints, worsening eyesight and a certain selective deafness, have marked the passage of her years. These, not wholly canine, inconveniences make for increasing dependency and occasional bewilderment, but for all that she's very fit and takes full advantage of a better than average quality of life.

Her palpable relief at being rescued, together with clear signs of less than kindly treatment at some point in her past, meant that we'd always been disinclined to consign her to boarding kennels while we were away. However, since she's a biddable little creature and never much trouble, and as our friends are willing victims, they, more-often than not, found her a temporary billet when we occasionally fled England to avoid wet summers, dark winters and widespread political gloom. Although our friends declared themselves happy to continue the arrangement, the combination of our early retirement and the evening of her years strongly recommended alternative plans for Darcey this time.

Giving up the daily grind (...*and the company car!*) had been celebrated with the purchase of a sleek, brand new convertible. For someone who had never before shown the slightest interest, my wife fell in love with it in the showroom at first sight and that, as they say, was that. The car, a stylish, dark blue, mean machine, came upholstered in ivory leather and was fitted with a racy matt black dashboard and appendages. Strangely, my wife took to posing in it as to the manor born so when, somewhat reminiscent of Toad of Toad Hall, I suggested an antique flying ensemble: fleece jackets; leather helmets; ancient goggles (*those with vertical splits in the glass*); and dashing white silk scarves, as suitable garb for the road, she was thoughtful for a long moment before dismissing the notion, but she hesitated. Make no mistake – the lady wavered!

Unlike other large purchases of the Those That Give Pause For Thought variety we never once suffered a hint of buyers' remorse but given the opportunity took to rationalising our extravagance: trips abroad; the top down; the wind in our hair; the dog in the back!

Another acquisition was a laptop computer purchased to satisfy a number of requirements. As well as serving as a backup to our principal desktop computer it was, and more to the point of this tale, obtained to provide a simple means of communication while we were away on our travels. In the event (*why am I not surprised?*) the

Internet and email capacity fell far short of the mark but because I am an incorrigible amender and polisher and my handwriting leaves much to be desired, the machine redeemed itself by serving as an admirable vehicle for this diary.

Ever grateful for the absence of television, we always take plenty of carefully selected books when travelling but for a change, I started writing this journal in the evenings, more-often after supper, tapping away with a glass of something motivating at my elbow. Frankly there were so many interesting, odd, or just plain silly events that affected us that we knew we wanted to preserve them to share with our friends or just fondly remember.

Other than for business appointments and their ilk, I'd never really disciplined myself to write a daily diary. Now, several days into the trip after I'd made the first notes and caught up with events, I found myself looking forward to the evenings and spare moments when, with more than a little help from my long suffering wife, I would dredge up the various incidents and reflections that had struck me as suitable to describe. Thus as time passed I found myself observing life's little foibles and disasters with a much more discerning eye and, whilst certainly not seeking to create events, I became tolerably better at identifying the experiences and scenes that hitherto I would have probably glossed over and in time, forgotten.

Towards the end of our journey the weather turned against us and this undoubtedly reduced the amount of available material. Indeed my early drafts included a large number of indifferent photographs - a clear sign of journalistic desperation.

Before our French odyssey we had already enjoyed a long weekend with Darcey on the Northumberland coast near Bamburgh, but the dress rehearsal was to take place in the West Country. Arrangements were made for a week in a dog friendly cottage low on Bodmin Moor to be closely followed by a long weekend's encore in the Welsh Marches. Firsts for us and in the event, trouble free, thoroughly agreeable experiences, characterised by picturesque locations and gracious hosts. Untroubled that is except for an unplanned excursion when, bewilderment temporarily overcoming navigation skills, poor Darcey wandered off on the moor and had to be found. This together with the sheer nuisance of dog hair spread liberally throughout our brand new car where, sticking like superglue, it resisted most methods of removal known to modern science. But to be fair - ever since a truly cringe inducing episode involving a formal dinner with a business colleague and his stylishly black velvet skirted partner; imprudent canine cuddles; a subsequent light coating of stark white dog hair; and a completely inadequate clothes brush - we've always known that a little Darcey goes a very, very long way.

Nevertheless, so far so good and at Christmas, with the dog torn between guarding the hearth and supervising proceedings, we lingered in the candlelight of our dress up dinner - a fine roast goose, winter vegetables and all the trimmings, with a very palatable bottle of deep red Chinon to wash it all down - while conversation hearkened back to summer's enjoyable adventures and the anticipation of further explorations in warmer climes. In and among the fruit and nutshells Provence beckoned.

Between pudding and the port we'd agreed to go - one

17

of life's easier decisions; thereafter plotting and planning commenced and Internet searches contrived to dominate the New Year. Thus it was that, with time and much effort, a passable itinerary emerged, one which seemed to satisfy, at least in most respects, the conflicting demands and constraints we house hunting amateur Grand Tourists had imposed upon ourselves. Dog friendly was a must and cottage breaks in France offered excellent prospects for that. We wanted to go soon for the sun and extra daylight, certainly not later than early spring. Having already ruled out suggestions of northern climes - far too dark and dank - the south of France seemed a natural destination. Then there were other questions; should we concentrate on one or two southern *départements* more or less chosen at random or extend our range much wider? If so, how far was enough to drive between stops? How long should we take? How *big* was France?

As it turned out a combination of range and residue almost foiled our ambitions and a fall at the first seemed a racing certainty. When we thought about it all our earlier trips had been in reach, that is to say drivable in a few hours, certainly less than a day, but journeying by car to the south of France would take at least three days and we would be using hotel and B&B lodgings *en route*. What would become of the dog? Although she's a good traveller we had no intention of consigning her to the car overnight in mid France - in mid February! Frankly, Darcey in the role of Little Orphan Annie had simply not occurred to us. Further, we wholeheartedly agreed that a repeated light coating of surplus dog hair was both socially and mechanically unacceptable.

A friend in our morning dog-walking gang solved the

accommodation problem.   Seizing the moment she discovered amongst her goods and chattels an elderly directory of dog friendly hotels and *pensions* in France, a practical source that was quickly updated and improved by means of the Internet.

All that then remained was the hair.

I well remember my father telling me of an old time Hampshire gamekeeper who followed the local hunt on a bicycle. He would have an unearthing spade tied to its handlebars and a working pair of Jack Russell terriers in a sack slung across his back; the dogs' heads sticking out with at least one peering over the old boy's shoulder, nose to the wind and ears flying in the breeze. Whilst we'd seriously considered a duffel bag or even a rucksack to contain the dog and her undisciplined coat, our local Tesco supermarket, sold us, at very competitive rates, a prefabricated collapsible dog carrier. The medium sized version, allegedly impermeable to dog hair, came equipped with a carrying handle on top, tropical fly screen side windows and zip fastened roller shutters at each end, the whole combination finished in shades of stylish brown.   It was inevitably christened *chez* Darcey by our friends and fitted neatly on the car's back seat. The Dog's opinion of these arrangements was not sought.

Demonstrating conviction and determination on my part Peter Mayle's humorous and informative best seller *A Year in Provence* reappeared at the bedside and as a source of further inspiration, the *Wayfarer's All* chapter of *Wind in the Willows* joined the collection.   I observed that while Ratty wavered, Peter succumbed to The Call of the South and so, albeit temporarily, would we.

Thus things progressed apace and our cunning plan could now be firmed up. Since we would be driving throughout we contrived to divide our travels into neat, fairly effortless, four hour legs and as the only absolutes comprised sailings and cottage bookings, much else was up for grabs. In the event overnight bed and breakfast stops for the trip out were remarkably easy to organize and just not required between the various cottage bookings, so this allowed a degree of flexibility, particularly for our eventual return to UK.

Soon emails and telephone calls commenced and before long additional folders appeared in the email programme to cope with all the enquiries. Eventually cheques and the Gold Card had secured our reservations and we were almost ready for the off.

Following the best military planning traditions our family expedition was arranged so as to contain outbound and inbound phases and at its heart, an extended southern France itinerary.

D Day was scheduled for Thursday the 14th of February.

14th February Continued

The outbound arrangements called for a simple, leisurely, four hour drive down to Kent for an overnight stay before sailing to Calais. Thereafter four hours on the *autoroute* to Langres, a little short of Dijon, for a second overnight stop, followed by a further four hour run to Vaison la Romaine for our first week's stay. Expected at our first cottage on the Saturday we'd booked passage from Dover on Friday morning's early ferry.

So off we set.   Wayfarers all.   I draw a discreet veil over our experience on the British motorway system. The whole ghastly nose to tail experience was relieved only by a quieter hour away from the mayhem on the toll section of the M6 motorway that bypasses Birmingham, in my view a very sensible thing to do.   The perfectly awful combination of European behemoths thundering along while vying with their lesser, home grown, cousins for possession of the entire carriageway and thus creating traffic jams of monstrous proportions, simply beggars belief.   As does I might add, the disgraceful practice, undoubtedly slipped in unnoticed by unscrupulous government ministers, of British distance - measured since ancient times in imperial miles and thus understood by all - now being signposted in questionable foreign kilometres.

…and so by stages, we arrived at a Bed and Breakfast farmhouse near Canterbury.

14th February   Crockshard Farm   Canterbury

Crockshard farmhouse nestles in a tranquil fold of the rolling Kent countryside near Canterbury.   Like many of its contemporaries it is an old, attractive, rather rambling building set in extensive grounds but long since shorn of the lands its yeoman farmers once worked.   There are riding stables and a gang of gregarious pigs to greet the visitor and a rather forlorn notice pleading that the door be kept shut to keep out the farm cats.   Entry *sans* cats is gained through a narrow whitewashed passage with muddy boots and hanging coats and damp rainproofs and boot scrapers and well used doormats, which opens into a wooden framed afterthought of a conservatory cum hall, with polished tiles and lush cultivated greenery and odd mysterious rooms off.

Business is transacted in the kitchen. This is a portmanteau space of epic proportions which, at its heart contains a cheerfully weather-beaten refectory table set for at least fifteen although it looked to have space for fifty with room to spare. A fitting place for the hunt breakfast or sun weary harvesters home from the fields and eager for ale and supper and here our hostess is discovered, laundering on an industrial scale.

We are expected and a comfortable bedroom is already allocated and Darcey fits in right away; so no change there. This whole house has a secure, loved, if slightly neglected air and the sitting room, with its log burner ablaze and many comfortable bagged out leather chesterfields gathered around, further demonstrates its charm. We feel at ease at Crockshard Farm. I even more so as a nubile daughter of the house, naked but for an only slightly adequate bath towel, sprints damply through the sitting room breathless apologies dripping in her wake. By way of explanation it's Valentine's night and her hair is yet to be done. We don't mind and neither, it appears, did she.

This is a happy home and we're pleased to be here. I discover later that our hostess, an anthropologist, gave up lecturing to restore this house to life and the result is a credit to her.

The farm only caters for bed and breakfast so the Griffin's Head in a nearby village is recommended for supper.

14th February The Griffin's Head Chillenden

If the Griffin's Head is not 18th century it certainly should be as it's exactly the sort of hostelry that could well have been written by Dickens.

Situated in a nearby village it is white without and mellowed brick within. Warmed by open log fires and cheerfully higgledy-piggledy, the Griffin's Head extends a cosy welcome beyond its generous car park.

We arrive shortly after dark and the bar is already full. Through the happy crush we order drinks and enquire as to the possibility of supper. Mine Host is desolate, we've not booked and as it's Saint Valentine's night, every swain and his sweetheart for miles about will be dining here tonight and just to prove the point many have arrived already. We are disappointed but brave - and our display of undernourished courage obviously wins hearts and friends so a table in the pub's farthest depths is discovered and prepared for us. Making our way over uneven worn brick floors we are shown through passages, past side rooms and unusual chambers with rather oddly ordered dining tables already set and lit. Shortly we arrive at our places and dine splendidly, albeit in splendid isolation. My wife's scallops melt, while my home-made pate is exactly as described, not too smooth and accompanied by a light chilli dressing, the combination of which is quite delicious. The roast *canard* is just so and the berry *jus* accompaniment a delight. We thoroughly enjoyed this meal; out of the ordinary pub grub lifted by its undoubted quality and presentation.

Unusually in this day and age the youngsters who make up the serving staff are a cheerful crowd, professional and enthusiastic, which says a lot for them and the pub's owners.

…and so to the farm and a good night's sleep.

15th February   Crockshard Farm Canterbury

This morning, after early dog walking, I am directed to repack the boot and in my unbridled eagerness forget the door, its dire warning and the cats, and so, task completed, I am escorted back to the kitchen by one of the outcasts. We take a light breakfast below the salt; the trespassing feline graciously occupying a carver at the head of the table looking for all the world as though Pharaoh Ramasses II is expected back soon.

…and so to Dover.

15th February   Dover and the Sea France Car Ferry

Now I'm no expert but compared with most British airports through which I've passed during my various travels, the Port of Dover seemed unusually well organized.

We are in good time and our ferry is delayed but not overly much, so there is plenty of time to buy a newspaper and start the crossword before boarding. Thus, after parking the car ready for the off, I endure a damp and squally route march to the terminal building, which on arrival, is no more than mildly chaotic. My hunched slog back is interrupted by a fluorescent marshal. Even though we've scrupulously kept to the walkways and pedestrian crossings, this jobsworth is determined to detain our straggling column of windswept pedestrians while simultaneously halting an intersecting queue of embarking trucks in order to check, in painstaking detail, each impatient driver's papers. Unloved and unsheltered, his increasingly desperate directions largely unheeded, he seemed to be the only participant in the game unmindful of the scornful derision emanating from the remaining players. A malevolent symptom of odious officialdom - if he weren't already there they'd simply have to invent him.

Once embarked our crossing was largely uneventful, as only a car ferry channel crossing can be. Deck hands briskly directed vehicles on board and off with surly abandon and scant regard for damage or discomfort. Fellow passengers were mostly inconsiderate, intolerant or in my way, and the professional truck driving fraternity, well versed in such passages, imperious.

Elsewhere the ship's crew all seemed to have been assigned supporting roles in a chorus of shop assistants and no one had thought to provide a cash machine. However, the excellent *café crème* and warm *croissants* restored my equilibrium.

By and large not a bad trip for thirty quid; the bankrupt Channel Tunnel costs over four times the price and has much less romance. You just don't set sail in a tunnel nor yet get to see Dover's White Cliffs recede into the murk.

…and so to France.

15th February   Calais

It is my considered opinion that Calais was rather better ordered when under the benevolent but firm control of medieval English lords.   The Bastard of Fauconburg[1] springs to mind.

Disembarkation *en* France was a fascinating experience involving several remarkable instalments. Almost by inspiration, much like swallows migrating south for the winter, a Great Escape to the car deck resulted in a mildly disorganized crush as the entire compliment of passengers attempted to get off all at once.   This interesting 'flocking' phenomenon, about which more later, took place without anybody actually looking anyone else in the eye or coming into contact, so folk shuffled along corridors, down steep interminable stairs and through the tiny watertight doors in a state of compressed carefulness.   The futility of this crush was soon apparent as, gaining the vehicles, their occupants were neither allowed to enter them or stand immediately nearby. This was puzzling, until, as if by magic, the deck suddenly dropped away and the cars, hitherto horizontal, now lay at an improbable downward angle.   We teeter to our car and are thankful for the handbrake.

The dog, condemned by The Rules to her house on the car's back seat for the voyage, awakes.   Blissfully detached she has slept through rough weather, the car alarm - which clearly considered that our vehicle was being hijacked mid channel - and variable geometry.

---

[1] Thomas Neville, the Bastard of Fauconburg (*1429 - 1471*)   Supporter of Richard Neville, Earl of Warwick - the Kingmaker.

In our turn we descend and remarkably free of loathsome bureaucracy, make landfall in France.

The satellite navigation machine - purchased at no little expense solely to anticipate the inevitable dramas and turbulences consequent on my wife's navigational dyslexia - is sulking, therefore I rely on the route signs and *quelle surprise!* am disgorged onto the Autoroute des Anglaise with a minimum of fuss. Darcey and my wife are unimpressed.

15th February Autoroute Pas de Calais and Champagne

Living up to its name the *autoroute* is awash with the British. UK car registration plates abound while the reputedly terrifying French motorists seem to have conceded the match - but no! My wife, for it must be she, has omitted to adjust the time. We are just ready for late morning coffee whilst all of France is preoccupied with *le dejeuner;* consequently all is peace and tranquillity. We head for Rheims and the south. The car behaves superbly and the kilometres tick by effortlessly. I venture that in the spirit of *Égalité et Fraternité* distance on the *autoroute* should be signposted in Imperial Miles. My wife is silent on the matter and Darcey is asleep.

As always I am struck by the excellent condition of motorways abroad. There is precious little litter, regular rest stops and service stations, and the well-behaved traffic flows evenly without the menacing assistance of numerous speed cameras. Perhaps the intrusive kilometre signs on the M6 will serve to improve matters?

It is easy to forget by how much agriculture dominates

the French countryside. On south-eastwards into Champagne across France's abandoned battlefield regions, empty countryside rolls away over vast well-tended fields, the landscape gradually changing becoming more rugged as we descend towards Dijon.

The plan is to make an overnight stop at one of the admirable Logis de France network of hotels in the village of Saints-Geosmes a little south of Langres.

Below Chaumont we leave the motorway and continue south past brooding Langres.

Dominating its hilltop, Langres' gloomy, weathered, stone clad ramparts, bastions and citadels command the countryside and with a jaundiced sergeant major's eye, well-sited gun ports defy us to slip by unnoticed on the ring road *Toutes Directions*.

Built on a promontory that dominates the river Marne, Andematunnum, then Ligones now Langres, stands as a one-time capital of the Gallic Ligones people. The Romans, ever the opportunists, seeing the site's strategic value first cultivated the tribe and then fortified their settlement. Throughout the Middle Ages the church continued the practice ensuring the town's prosperity and developing and strengthening its defences. With the Renaissance came increased affluence and a programme of public building alongside the military that then included a dozen towers and some seven gates. By now obsolete, never really having heard a shot fired in anger, Langres' city walls and fortifications continued to be developed well into the 19th century. That defensive redundancy was revised somewhat by a sharp spat in September 1944 when Nazi occupation was ended, appropriately enough by French troops of General Truscott's US VI Corps, part of the Dragoon force advancing northwards up the Rhône valley in support of D Day's Overlord landings.

Beyond, through clearly redundant monumental gates, their triumphs long forgotten, we enter interminable ranks of brooding Empire style, barracks. Long abandoned they parade still, garbed in peeling field grey, lining both sides of the road. Neglected, boarded and shuttered their war is done as, like the old soldiers they once housed, they just fade away.

These places hold a fascination for me and I always intend to discover more about them but alas I almost never do. As we later discovered, Langres' brine and annatto washed cheese thoroughly deserves it reputation but we reserved judgement on its decision to twin with Beaconsfield, considering Aldershot - Home of the British Army welcomes careful drivers, a far better and probably more appropriate choice.

15th February   Saints-Geosmes Champagne Ardenne

Saints-Geosmes is but a pace away and the Jumeaux hotel awaits us. The Auberge des Trois Jumeaux had been selected for compelling reasons. Whilst obeying our four hour drive rule, it lays roughly midway between Calais and Vaison la Romaine and it is dog friendly. The dog sleeps on.

This is a tiny traditional village, dominated by its church and *mairie*, with but one main street which is now largely redundant due to the advent of a bypass where *modern* business is to be found, and here, after only two false starts, we discover the hotel. Darcey awakes; I park the car; my wife makes enquiries within.

Monsieur is *désolé*. There are, he explains, two Jumeaux hotels in Saints-Geosmes and we are expected at the other establishment, which is to be found in the centre of the village. If *Madame* would but stand on tiptoe and look thus she will undoubtedly see the rear of the building. *Madame* does and having so done, we set off for another tour of Saints-Geosmes.

Once again Logis de France does us proud. Our room is comfortable and very well appointed, the service first-rate and dinner is served between 7:30 and 10:00 pm.

At 8:00 pm the hotel's restaurant is not full, in fact it is almost empty but even so a table has been reserved for us. A Standard French Family, mother, father and two well-mannered young children, occupy a nearby table and we are reminded how common it is to see generations of families in France eating together and how well behaved and well-informed even quite young children are when dining out.

Our dinner is accompanied by an entertainment. We decide to investigate the mysteries of the twenty-three Euro menu. *Monsieur* cocks an eyebrow - a wise choice! Most of the dishes on offer are familiar but I am intrigued by *Rognon de Veau a l'ancienne*. What delight could this be? My wife enquires. *Monsieur* is at a loss but is evidently a Charades aficionado and in the very best traditions of that party game and a certain linguistic desperation, presents a mime. We are expectant.

The first word; an animal, so tall, with horns - thus!

30

This closely followed by what can best be described as fantasy samurai *seppuku* - a grimace of clearly agonising, ritual disembowelment.

Enlightenment! It's veal!

The undisputed master of the game, Lionel Blair, would have been so proud - although I considered Mooing well outside the scope and spirit of the rules.

Now I know that it's just not politically correct, but I happen to like escallops of veal so with mouth-watering anticipation we order.

The tiny kidneys *sautéed* to perfection and served in a white pepper sauce are delicious especially with a rather good Côtes du Rhône. I pause to contemplate the standard of French education and anatomy lessons.

…and so to bed.

16th February   Burgundy and Rhône Alpes

Early next morning the car is covered in several centimetres of frost and having de iced and repacked our luggage and the dog, we depart but only after *Madame* has presented my wife with a copy of the new Logis guide as her prize.

Back on the *autoroute* continuing south, we arrive at Dijon in no time at all.   Whilst I've always been impressed by its mustard, we sail serenely by and, apart for the rather good tourist road signs, are amazed by a complete lack of having been anywhere at all.   It seems to me that continental motorways are like that, either feast or famine and so to the *smorgasbord* that is Lyon.

Originally a city created for pensioned off Roman legionaries, the River Rhône and the motorway bisect Lyon and industry infects the wounds. Brash light commerce and frenetic business crowds our route - where we are particularly struck by one enterprising car dealer, boasting by way of advertisement, a four square, glass encased, colour coordinated tower of two-seater Smart Cars stacked one above the other at least ten stories high. I was led to wonder how on earth this multicoloured modern day ziggurat was assembled …and what if *Madame* demands *that* particular Smart Car? It would be like manipulating a gigantic Rubik's Cube to get the damn things down. The dog is asleep again.

Departing Lyon the Rhône is crowded by heavier industry, port facilities and oil refineries, with gaudy storage tanks cheek by jowl lining the carriageway; a hideous modern monument to our peripatetic society. Driving past I am momentarily overcome with guilt but the feeling soon passes - as do the offending installations.

Later we start to climb. The temperature is noticeably warmer, at least the dashboard instrument says so and the verges are lush with evergreen hedges and cypresses. The town of Orange is ahead and we have arrived in Provence.

Chapter Three

Touring the South of France

Provence

Greeks and Gauls, Romans, Germanic Merovingians and Carolingians, counts and popes, writers, painters, soldiers and politicians have all succumbed and surrendered to the allure of Provence ...and the attraction? Today's visitor might name, wonderful hot summers, pleasing wines of colourful style and variety - diverse reds and whites and elegant *rosé*.

Fabulous dishes of chicken, lamb and goat and terrific terrines of game. Wonderful Mediterranean fish and crustaceans; *Bouillabaisse*, sardines, *Oursinade*, *Brandade de Morue*, The superb vibrant diversity of vegetables of wonderful freshness, crisp salads dressed with olive oil. Garlic, olives, *aioli*, *tapenade*, *rouille*, *ratatouille* and of course the fruit: grapes, peaches, melons, apricots, cherries. Heady wild herbs; sage, rosemary, fennel, thyme, basil and lavender.

Oak and Truffles. Surprisingly cold winters; the Mistral and the Marin, thick stews of game, chicken, pork and beef, *daube provençal*. Tarts, *gateaux* and breads.

The Rhône and Camargue. Scrubby Garrigue, mountains, massifs, and limestone Calanques. Bouches-du-Rhône, the Var, the Alpes-Maritime, Alpes-de-Haute-Provence, Vacluse. Pastis and Pétanque.

Weather culture and landscape - unique Provence!

The Rhône valley

Distinguished by its harsh winters and hot summers the northern Rhône valley is significantly less warm than it's southern partner consequently its mix of viniculture is different. Syrah (*aka Shiraz*) grapes predominate and as I was soon to rediscover, its red wines have a typical green olive or smoked bacon nose. I'm fond of French plonk, particularly Côtes du Rhône and over time I've come to appreciate that it's drinking the stuff where it's made that makes the difference. Hindsight is a wonderful thing because frankly, that is a lesson relearned.

During one gorgeous autumn, the sort of Indian summer that only seems to exist in memory, my army unit decamped to exercise in the Rhineland's Moselle valley below Koblenz. Now, and with the benefit of age experience and it must be admitted, a certain duplicity, it is abundantly clear to me that the brigade's somewhat less than tactical venture down the length of the river's *Moselwinestrasse*, exactly one hundred and eighty degrees in the wrong direction, rather than rehearsing to stem a Cold War communist invasion, was undertaken solely to take advantage of and delight in, the region's October wine festival. Unfortunately and to the commanding brigadier's obvious outrage, no one in the headquarters had thought to bring a corkscrew. Thus are wars lost and junior officers' careers ruined.

Striking east through the vineyard carpeted valleys we begin a gentle climb up to our first destination.

A frisson of excitement - the dog is awake!

16th February   Vaison la Romaine
Le Clos Du Quenin

The charming town of Vaison la Romaine, set in the hills just north east of Orange above the Rhône Valley, is a slightly uncomfortable juxtaposition of the modern and antique.

Our triumphal entry into this rediscovered ancient Roman town goes largely unremarked and unheralded. I'm fairly sure there should be a slave, garbed in white, holding aloft a victor's laurel chaplet, to whisper dread warnings of mortality and the ephemeral nature of glory into my ear.   Over my shoulder the dog pants.

We have taken a property on the pretty gated Le Clos Du Quenin estate for a week and first impressions are favourable but before we can settle in, a game for two players with gates, doors, keys and wall safe combinations must be played.   Well before the half time whistle one side retires with hurt feelings and parking and unpacking may commence.

Le Clos etc., named for an historical cleric, lies on the northern outskirts of the modern town and comprises a couple of dozen or so of the dwellings that are bought as investments - either to rent or as holiday homes.   They are simply not the sort of houses one would buy to actually live in, and are furnished accordingly, but for a week and as a base of operations this house is fine and we take up temporary occupancy.

As we are by now seasoned campaigners settling in does not take over long and reconnaissance of Vaison commences.   Soon an outline the town has been mentally mapped and provisions and other necessities sourced.   The car is washed and tidied after which we repair to the house to draw breath only to discover that age and neglect having taken their toll, we are no longer up to driving a little less than a thousand miles in four days without suffering the consequences. Wine is opened; a rest day is declared and further operations suspended *pro tempore.*

17th February   Le Clos Du Quenin

Rest and recuperation continues.   Darcey encourages me to explore the local walks in the surrounding area.   A nearby hillside is preferred; a lonely spot but good steep walking for us and almost reminiscent of our own Pennine hillside but with vines.

Later my wife and I take a late Sunday luncheon in Vaison's restaurant of choice.   The weather is bright but cold so we select a table within.   The waiter brings the menu inscribed on tablets like biblical Commandments but written in lurid chinagraph pencil.   We eat barbecued king prawn salad with slices of local ham and a home made dressing, followed by succulent rare roasted noisettes of lamb crusted with herbs.   Delicious!

After lunch there follows a brief initial inspection of part of the Roman excavations, which we decide, whilst interesting and definitely photogenic, look exactly like the Roman excavations we've seen elsewhere in Sussex, Northumberland and Israel, so we opt for more well deserved R&R and head home to Le Clos etc.

18th February   Dancing at Avignon

'Sur le pont d'Avignon
L'on y danse,   l'on y danse,
Sur le pont d'Avignon
L'on y danse,   tous en rond.'
Traditional French folk song

It seems that the shepherd boy Bénézet was commanded by angels to bridge the Rhône at Avignon and felt the need to lift massive stones just to prove the point.   Lacking the means if not the strength, his example inspired wealthy local sponsors to fund the project and forming a guild of Bridge Brothers, they no doubt gained religious indulgences and increased trade. Like many well intentioned, one might venture, divinely inspired, projects it suffered regular collapses.   After becoming increasingly rickety the bridge was abandoned following a severe flood in 1668 and of its original 22 arches only four now stand.   The by now Saint Bénézet was buried in a small chantry on the bridge; the various fates of his several backers can be guessed at.

The medieval citizens of Avignon may well have danced in a circle on, or as the Guide Michelin has it, on the island beneath, Bénézet's bridge.   As for us, arriving in the late morning, we simply could not find parking space within or without the city and therefore demonstrated *fraternité* by driving round and around the ring road while admiring the battlements and bastions.

The city boasts highly photogenic, albeit badly designed, ramparts built to defend a papal palace where the French pontiffs and later schismatic anti-popes held court.   Rather like the Curate's Egg, having endured inappropriate contemporary building alongside the medieval, Avignon is good in parts and, in common with so many other historic cities, it is, it seems to me, in very real danger of being overtaken by the demands of an unsympathetic modern society; one largely intolerant of its city's place in history. I really don't deny the need for new building and city development but yearn for more sensitivity in construction and location.

Our appetites whetted, we determine not to be defeated and shall make an effort to revisit Avignon - *Cité des Papes* before heading south at the end of the week.

The drive back to Vaison is across country and again we are struck by the beauty of the Rhône valley with its multitude of regimented vineyards, ordered orchards, pleated lavender fields and gnarled olive groves. Pines and evergreen hedges mark the way and here and there Cypresses form full stops.

Frankly we'd always imagined this week to be a break from driving down but there's so much to see that we shall be hard pressed to fit everything in.

🐾 🐾

We finally arrive back in Vaison in the late afternoon and pop to the supermarket to buy a paper. Before heading off I ask my wife if she's noticed anything. No she has not. I try another tack. Surely something significant is apparent on the front page, perhaps the date? Ah…! It's my birthday. I am sixty-two years old today and this non-milestone celebration of endurance and survival has been overlooked, forgotten, lost, ignored. Ignored I say! There is not even a trace of embarrassment at this gross oversight to be seen.

Someone's going to suffer for this omission.

Returning to Le Clos etc, Darcey at least is pleased to see me and with tail wagging, dances *tous en round* but fails to provide cake. That's the Dogs' Home out of the Will!

On dogs and the responsibilities of being owned by them

Being *en vacance* in someone else's house makes the dog owner's life just a little more difficult. It's not as if you can let the poor animal out into the back garden any time that nature calls. There might not even be a back garden, suitable or otherwise. *Non*! One is required to be more circumspect and a degree of thought is required so as not to offend one's absentee host and the neighbours. A routine must be established and suitable convenient canine toilet alternatives to the back garden found. It is my experience that acquaintanceships with like-minded souls are struck up when so engaged.

Madame is the custodian of a bumptious wire-haired terrier of indeterminate parentage and, while the dogs do what it is that dogs do when meeting, we converse. On reflection I think that conversation is much too strong a word to describe the *englench* with which we communicate. Madame is clearly more comfortable with her schoolgirl English than I with my smatterings of army French so *franglaise* is clearly out. We chatter on a while comparing breeds and bemoaning the weather and exchange a surprising amount of information.

19th February   A trip to the Lubéron
Ménerbes and Bonnieux

Ever since reading Peter Mayle's books I'd always wanted to visit the Lubéron.   Not simply as homage or to seek The House, or indeed the incredible cast of characters who populate his books, but rather the landscape and the scenery and frankly it does not disappoint.   We drive down on the motorway and turn left at Cavaillon and it's as simple as that.

Following the quiet minor roads up to Bonnieux past Ménerbes on its hill and the huge forested limestone rise of the mountains to the south, Mayle's valley is a fertile verdant empty scene the odd wisp of wood smoke drawn lightly against the green.

I thought I understood the attraction; now I'm sure of it.   Of course things are never entirely as one imagines. I'd failed to grasp quite how hilly the hill villages actually are, and how steep and how close the land rises to the south, but the vineyards and oaks and forests were to be found just as written.   I'm pleased we went.

No doubt once folk at home realize that we've visited Ménerbes fellow enthusiasts will ask about *chez* Mayle but since we didn't seek it out I'm afraid they will just have to live with disappointment.

20th February   Ascending Mount Ventoux

It's a grey day at Le Clos etc.   Our speck of Provence is overcast but this fails to prevent a few billion Euros worth of the French air force performing thunderous passes over the valley in flocks.

We rise late and muddle into town for a delayed *café crème* in a bar the like of which I would have been pleased to have been thrown out of in my earlier days. Drinking my coffee I am strongly reminded of those bleak soldiers' bars, to be found the world over, where everything fragile or vulnerable has been removed or long since broken.

As a young military policeman in the 1960s I was stationed in the Cameron Highlands of Pahang, Malaysia - an attractive, almost village constable lifestyle, in the British Army's popular change of air station, where troops and their families could enjoy a short break to escape the lowland's tropical heat and oppressive humidity. Normally an undemanding one-man post, at an ungodly hour I received an urgent call to a similarly barren bar in the village.

All authority without and trepidation within, I arrived to discover the Chinese lady owner outraged, near to tears and fearful for her license. Inside a platoon of the Royal New Zealand Regiment's finest were noisily engaged in drinking the place dry, having first created and now determinedly defending to last man, a small alp of carefully stacked empty Tiger Beer tins. Clearing this echoing barn of drunken soldiers, recently returned from combat in Vietnam and anticipating a well deserved R&R, was going to take more than a little imagination and determination.

In the wings, hanging for grim death to the bar, I spotted a gently intoxicated NCO. For want of more appropriate conversation I suggested that, it being two in the morning, he might stand me a drink for my trouble and in the way of all things New Zealand, this beer rapidly turned into a pair, possibly more.

Having now made friends and influenced people, it only remained to manoeuvre the equivalent of something the size and weight of an affable All Blacks' pack out into the street and back to their camp, a couple of miles or so distant. My patrol car was a mere Leyland Mini and if you've ever heard the hoary old joke about how to get four elephants into a Mini (*two in the front and two in the back*) you'll have no difficulty in appreciating the next problem. Eventually, with the car full to bulging and various arms, legs and other anatomy protruding, a body draped over the bonnet and another on the roof - I steered while the remainder of the happy scrum pushed the groaning vehicle and its cheerful, if rather compressed, occupants uphill to the barracks.

Later that week the now perfectly behaved Kiwis invited my wife and I and a flurry of pretty nurses, to a *Pork and Puha* farewell luncheon. This feast comprised pit cooked pork with assorted greens and cabbage and required copious amounts of beer, setting a fire and digging a large hole in the commanding colonel's immaculate and much loved putting green, in order to bury hot rocks and steam the palm leaf wrapped food. Our hosts returned to the war in Vietnam before this small outrage was discovered, thus official retribution could be not be contemplated and dire military repercussions were not visited upon them. I can only hope they survived.

Here in Vaison the coffee is excellent and *Monsieur* and his clientele surprisingly warm. We shall come here again.

As the morning progresses more of the town and its remarkably well-preserved Roman remains are scrutinized and I muse that ancient buildings seem so small when excavated and reconstructed. Like the Le Clos etc., cottage it's a mini world; one in which I should forever be knocking elbows or barking my shins.

We are suddenly at a loss; the morning has gone and map in hand we're in debate for an afternoon's activity. It's one of those 'Shall we shan't we' moments, so I take a lead and suggest a leisurely drive to Mount Ventoux, a neighbouring beauty spot and the source of much local pride. Although it's some thirty kilometres distant the mountain forms a prominent and substantial background to Vaison. It's a view that Darcey and I admire every morning from our adopted vineyard.

On Flocking

We return to the car which I have carefully parked smack bang in the middle of the town's sizeable but less busy upper car park. No one has parked beside us, which is remarkable, for I have a theory about car parks, one that deserves a word or two of explanation.

First, it should be noted that I have a low tolerance of that portion of car owning society who are careless about the minor damage they regularly inflict on other people's vehicles. Irrespective of inbuilt plastic defence and ramparts of rubbing strips these individuals will find a way to scrape and dent other folk's bodywork with monotonous regularity ...and, mark my words, they are not always the drivers of the oldest scruffiest car on the park. Oh no! Negligent Dinkers and Dingers are to be found among all classes of drivers.

Second, I subscribe to 'The Flocking Habits of Man Theory.' This hypothesis, as recently reported in the Daily Telegraph, (*so it must be true*) is the subject of some interesting recent academic work which suggests that when purposeless, mankind will tend to group around anyone who appears purposeful. This is so whether or not the person flocked around actually has a purpose or not. They merely have to look the part.

I offer two examples: some years ago, in those halcyon days when Elton John and Kiki Dee declined to break each other's hearts and consequently topped the hit parade, I was a military police platoon commander in Germany and was ordered to preserve Britain and NATO's interests whilst a *Bundeswehr* Leopard tank and its crew alighted at a nearby British military railway yard. The tank would then be driven onto a tank transporter vehicle to continue its journey by road. No problem there you might think.

At the appointed time forty odd tons of tank disembarked from its flatbed rail car, squealing and crunching down a ramp into the marshalling area as though born to it. The marshalling yard, designed and constructed to deal with hundreds of such events simultaneously, was vast and exactly in its centre stood a substantial concrete structure which housed, if memory serves, emergency electrical points and the like. The concrete block, the Leopard tank and my Land Rover were the only objects for at least half a mile in any direction. With an *élan* wholly befitting this worthy successor to the *Panzer Korps*, the young German commander ordered 'Full Speed Astern' or whatever it is that tank commanders do, and unerringly, some might argue inevitably, collided full tilt with the concrete block. This chap would never make a Rommel - but his example serves admirably to demonstrate both the Flocking and Dinging theories.

More recently we took to using the Vaison upper car park so as to park our lovely new car apart from other vehicles - potential Dingers every one. Each time we returned to find that we'd been 'flocked' around whilst the remainder of the huge park was empty. Incredible!

🐕 🐕

The road up Mount Ventoux is picturesque and steep, with many exciting hairpin bends and views of the limestone rock outcrops through lovely, well-managed woods and scrub dotted with wild herbs. We take it easy so as to enjoy the experience and are followed from below by a small black Ford Escort, clearly having the same thing in mind.

Not far from the summit at a place I know, there is an observation area, mostly a large lay by with signpost maps and the like, where we pull in to take photographs. The black Ford pulls in and parks behind us.

Within our car we find our cameras and prepare for photography when moments later, accompanied by an aggressive roar, much scattering of gravel and contemptuous scowls, the Ford and its indignant occupants accelerates past and burns rubber on up the mountain road.

Flocked again! It never fails.

21st February   Clinging to the Gorges de l' Ardèche

For a hole in the ground the Ardèche Gorge has much to recommend it.   It's a brilliantly sunny day, just why we're here.   Clear and bright and definitely not the sort of day to waste inspecting, whatever their respective merits, various *provençal* ruins: churches; castles; or country houses.

A nice aspect of cottage holidays are the brochures and guide books previous inhabitants leave to assist their less knowledgeable followers and at Le Clos etc., they have recommended the gorge and who are we to ignore such intrepid trailblazing advice.   With car top down and GPS machine instructed we set off to the village of Vallon Pont d'Arc at the head of the gorge.   Frankly the couple of hours spent driving there is fairly uninspiring.   This trip is at my wife's suggestion and we are both disappointed to arrive at Vallon having done nothing more exciting than climb the far side of the Rhône valley and drink a *café crème* on the way.

I switch off the map reading machine and turn the car to head for home and almost immediately spot the road sign for the Ardèche Gorge's Tourist Route that has been lurking unseen in ambush.

'Courage mes enfants! Are we not tourists?   Is this not the tourist route?   What are we waiting for?   In the Cameron Highlands; thirty-three miles of steeply climbing hairpin bends through tropical heat and secondary jungle from Tapah Road up to Tanah Rata - driven regularly with panache and never a qualm.   Do we not frequently holiday in Mallorca?   The steep mountain climb from

46

Inca up to Lluc and Sollier - easy peasy! Was I not the intrepid adventurer who scaled Mount Ventoux but yesterday?'

The Ardèche Gorge is ancient. It is a prehistoric, steep sided, meandering cleft in a limestone plateau, remote enough to have been regularly lost to mankind. In comparison with other wonders of the world its dimensions are not vast but it has a primeval and dangerous feel. The tourist trail climbs steeply upwards and clings high on the cliffs' edge - and so do we. The sheer scree based cliffs are awe inspiring and the river glitters blue and bends its way far below. The only comfortable beings here are particoloured goats that emerge to beg for tit bits at the least excuse. Like all goats they have a faintly manic look; well to live here they would have to be barking, or in their case bleating, mad.

If you've ever seen the Michael Caine and Noël Coward film *The Italian Job* you'll remember the scene where Caine's sports car tumbles and smashes down an alpine cliff crashing to utter destruction. This austere abyss is steeper and deeper and more exposed and the brink is not well protected. There be precipices here and I for one am going to be very, very careful until we reach ground level again. The Ardèche Gorge is heart stopping in parts; definitely not a place for either the blase or the faint hearted - and certainly not to be missed.

We eventually descend emerging at Pont St Esprit, which is utterly unremarkable, apart from a stop for lunch that once again is quite excellent. We select a passable roadside cafe for no other reason than it's there and we can park easily and, recommendation being by far the best reference, customers aplenty, mainly families

47

and businessmen, are already eating.   Frankly, after that gorge I am ready to stop.

Our *entrée* is a self-service cold buffet apart from the olives, which are unexpectedly fiery with chilli and delicious.   My wife enjoys *bifteck bleau* whilst my *plat* is a braised blood sausage, promptly christened Pudding Noir, accompanied by Dijon mustard and served with *pommes de terre puree*.   Black pud and mash just doesn't have quite the same elegance.   With two glasses of beer I am soundly defeated before the dessert.

Three generations of a family are lunching alongside and once again we observe the normality of these events in France.   This particular family is owned by a young Jack Russell who, from his position beneath their table, graciously accepts occasional tit bits from above while maintaining good order and military discipline.

We return to Vaison to think about tomorrow.   We leave on Saturday so must pack up and tidy the house ready to depart.   It would be nice to see the Cathedral before we go and we'll take a decent lunch so that our evening will be free for last minute bits and pieces.

22nd February   Farewell to Le Clos Du Quenin

Today has been a day for administration.   Today is also a day that started badly when, early this morning, I slipped on the stairs and it being a chap thing, let the world know about it.   My wife thinks I'm a wimp.   The dog woke up!

We've packed and tidied the car and discovered that Darcey's Tesco supermarket house has completely fulfilled expectations, as there's hardly a trace of hair to be seen in the car; so something's turned out right today.

On recycling and the management of rubbish

I am responsible for the disposal of rubbish this morning. The Le Clos etc., estate has a locked room adjacent to its entrance gates which is dedicated to the collection of household rubbish with many huge colour coded bins and threatening multilingual posters, warning the unwary that they misdispose of carefully categorized rubbish at their peril. The whole thing works on an airlock principle in which the residents enter from inside the estate to dispose of their rubbish and the town's dustmen enter from the outside to collect it. How on earth will they be given their Christmas boxes? Strangely enough in what is a predominately wine-producing district there's no bin for the empties.

On the way to the garage for fuel we stop at the bottle bank where I am astonished at the amount of wine my wife and the dog have drunk.

Tomorrow we leave Vaison and head towards Le Beausset just above the coast to the east of Marseilles. We've enjoyed our week here. The weather has been mostly good and considering it was always to be a break from the haul down it's been quite busy.

Chapter Four

Provence

23rd February   Le Beausset   Les Lavendes
L'Enclos de La Daby

This is another family spot that's obviously much loved. Although the English owners are not in residence it has a very similar feel to Crockshard Farm and we've settled in right away.

The drive down to Le Beausset was a pleasure. We got away just a little ahead of schedule and even though it was Saturday the motorways were fairly clear.

On the matter of tolls

At Lançon, somewhat further south on the Autoroute du Soliel traffic paused at the toll.   As a verb 'paused' hardly does this event justice: traffic bunched; it jammed; it tailed back; conditions caused drivers to flock and since the flocking behaviour was abnormal and imposed and thus unsettling, French tempers frayed.   The toll itself is a massive structure with a vaguely Third Reich feel which spans the motorway and has no other apparent function than to form a mud-coloured concrete backdrop to the toll booths.   Lined up across the carriageways these are, unlike their monstrous stage set, loosely reminiscent of the starting gates at Ascot but possessing much less style.   All in all an ideal venue for *ad hoc* strife.   For whatever reason but undoubtedly closely related to Heathrow's erratic baggage handling software, the procedure broke down, as did any sense of traffic discipline.   Normally a fairly free-flowing system, things simply ground to a crawl with intermittent stops.   When eventually we neared the pay points matters improved, mind you by then the chaos was largely behind us, but the uproar continued unabated with a symphony for massed horns bellowing around the hillsides.   Oh joy!   Oh bliss!   Oh poop-poop!   Toady would have loved it.

I was struck by the dramatic change of scenery as we drove into the wild grey mountains and massifs that are the hinterland of the French coast above Marseilles and as I eulogise we pause at yet another motorway toll. We're getting quite used to these by now - in fact you can ask us anything.   My wife is officer-in-charge *autoroute* tickets and toll payments and I find it prudent to remember that at all times.   On finals and committed to landing it appears that the ticket has been misplaced. Frantic scrabbling about and much searching of bags and the car ensues before one of us realises that this is not the end of a section where payment is due but a prepay toll which, in the manner of all such apparatus, is patiently awaiting my wife to throw two Euro coins into the money bucket.   There is no ticket, lost or otherwise.   Coins are found and payment is made with what I considered rather bad grace.   I struggle to keep a straight face and stare ahead contemplating the rising barrier and the state of traffic.   It's going to be my fault.   It being a girl thing I can tell that Darcey's on my wife's side!   I just know that it's going to be my fault.

Then at last the sea.   The motorway turns east and sweeps above a bay and the glittering blue Mediterranean lies before us.   The sun is shining and all's right with the world.

🐏 🐏

L'Enclos de La Daby is tucked away in an amphitheatre of pinewoods above the town.   Like the field systems hereabouts, it is steeply terraced with retaining dry stone walls and trodden paths forming a patchwork among the trees.   The air is scented by the pines and antique gnarled olive tree stumps - looking like hewn grey trolls emerging from a carpet of pine needles - sprout renewed vigorous ash green growth from their devastated foundations.

The entrance to the estate is a track, which is a rugged, washed out affair and I fear for the suspension, but with much care and cursing and blaming of others, we arrive *en bois,* so to speak.

There are four separate cottages, of varying proportion and design, spread about the large wooded site with a charming swimming pool and stone laid patio at its centre.   We'd opted for the Les Lavendes holiday cottage, which, at first sight, looks like some peasant's hovel set in a Brothers Grimm forest.   Hearts sinking we discover the keys and enter.   It's quite nice.   In fact it's very nice with shutters and tiles, a wonderful open log fireplace, well appointed kitchen and a generous bathroom - in fact the whole is considerably more than the sum of its parts.   Out in the woods cut logs are stacked and there is another covered supply laid beside the cottage, with yet more arranged snug inside in a drying compartment above the hearth.

By now it's late afternoon and getting chilly so,

deploying my very best *Scouting for Boys* technique, I set a roaring welcome fire and shortly the cottage is filled with acrid choking smoke. Unlike the wonderfully scented wood smoke drawn of fiction, this malevolent fog clings and blinds and suffocates. We are forced outdoors.

Heroically I volunteer to re-enter so, breathless from a burning throat and squinting through half closed streaming eyes I open and shut combinations of doors and windows to create a draft and thus ameliorate matters. Sadly there is no improvement until my wife, who has experience in such matters, suggests that my inferno is placed too far forward on the hearth and should be sited much further back so as to enable the cloying miasma to draw up the chimney. Now it's well known that fire lighting is a chaps' thing and I am therefore sceptical but fearing a catastrophe, am now ready to try anything. Employing a handy shovel I push the blaze: logs; cinders; flame; sparks and smoke, towards the rear of this miniature Circle of Hell. The fire promptly draws perfectly. My wife is henceforth appointed officer-in-charge fires and I find it prudent to remember that at all times.

We enjoy an early supper with thick slices of delicious cold quiche and drink a smooth dark Morgon whilst sitting outside, the dog at my feet, in the late afternoon sun. A thin scribble of acid blue wood smoke drifts through the dark pines and perfumes the air.

24th February   Le Beausset

It's a grey Sunday morning and I explore the estate with Darcey. Together we inspect the shuttered cottages and nearby neighbours' properties while Le Beausset's church bells call the faithful to mass. Between the olive trees bulbs have established themselves and although no English bluebell bank, individual muscari, narcissus, hyacinth and wild orchids peep coyly up at us.

Lunch is taken in a rather nice and clearly popular, *Centre Ville* hotel restaurant, Le Relaise de la Caleche, in earlier times a post house. Its large, tall, made over dining room boasts a huge version of our cottage hearth and comes equipped with all the implements of a medieval kitchen, but much less smoke. Our waiter is anxious for us to occupy a pavement table in the hostelry's narrow roadside conservatory and to try his language skills, nevertheless we choose a table indoors and select our meal from English language menus, which I think is rather akin to ignoring the chopsticks and opting for cutlery in a Chinese restaurant.

The process of ordering a meal in France intrigues me. This Sunday morning many couples and families are dining but before their order can be taken, frequent and lengthy conversations take place with the waiters and in one individual case the owner, who answer prolonged questions and offer considered but protracted advice. I suggest to my wife that We English do not succumb to this plainly Gallic vice but are brisk when we consider the menu and having made up our minds, order our lunch with conviction and resolve. She smiles a withering smile and reminds me of my recent Saints-Geosmes' performance. I study the wine list and enquire at length about the *plat de jour.*

In what can best be described as Freudian slips, my wife starts with a combination of smoked and fresh salmon salad while I select the *canard fumé* with apple. The tender thinly sliced smoked duck goes so well with the tart slivers of fresh apple and crisp green salad although *mea culpa*, I am a little heavy handed with the olive oil. Thus I dab and dry after each mouthful while my wife acclaims the fish.

Her chicken with grapes and rice is hailed a triumph while my lamb shank, somewhat lacking imagination, is accorded silver gilt status. An anonymous *vin de pays rouge* is delicious and it takes much effort not to order a second carafe.

For dessert and because she's losing weight, my wife orders profiteroles. On arrival these delicacies are the size of plump pillows lounging on well padded, iced cream mattresses, swathed with a glossy quilt of melted dark chocolate, all surrounded by a whipped cream valance. Because I am also dieting and brave, I abstain and drink espresso, but eventually succumb and like a thief in the night, pilfer an occasional index finger-full of her whipped cream.

While my wife settles the bill I stroll to the nearby supermarket where I have parked the car and, as I subsequently discover, having failed to follow my clear instructions, she follows me out to the car park. Meanwhile and blissfully unaware of this disobedience, I drive to the hotel and park stylishly in the road outside to collect her. In the very best of French tradition I manage to block all the traffic and whilst so doing observe in the rear view mirror my wife advancing determinedly from some distance behind. Somewhat strangely after such a good and relaxing lunch she appears somewhat flushed, even unhappy.   Perhaps it is indigestion?   Entering the car rather loudly she hands me my spectacles, which I'd left in the restaurant.   I drive to Les Lavendes quietly.

In the afternoon I doze energetically in front of the fire and so does the dog.

25th February   Reflecting at Les Lavendes

Another dull day and whilst we take time to catch up on a few organizational matters with visits to butcher, baker, candlestick maker and newspaper vendor *et al*, I have time for reflection.

Graffiti

There is an unpleasant rash of graffiti in France. Meritless, unoriginal and intrusive, it occupies any and all surfaces and is a repetitious pastiche.   I'd have more sympathy if any of it were novel or less frequent.   The spray-painted fonts are predictable and thus tedious and there is no apparent message and as far as I can tell it is a pestilence spread throughout the country from Calais to Marseilles.

Boy racers

Motorcycles bore me and often so do their owners. Everywhere we go in towns and villages incredibly young boys wearing brand new, hugely outsized, glossy helmets occupy favoured street corners and pose astride or alongside their colourful elderly contraptions.   There appear to be two classes of machine, the off-road bike and the commuter's scooter and all sport L-plates. In both categories the youthful riders posture between frenetic bouts of activity when, racing about the streets sounding much like a wasp in a dustbin turned up to the highest possible volume, they scare old ladies into the gutters.

Strangely young French girls don't appear to play a part in the ritual and mostly the youths seem intent on paying court to each other. Sometimes the young men do not grow out of this adolescent phase and stout adults who really should know better, are to be seen, *sans* L-plates, adopting wholly unsuitable aerodynamic racing lines on incredibly noisy machines that are far too young, far too slow, and far, far too small.

The crossword

Trips abroad just wouldn't be tolerable without the Daily Telegraph's crossword. In this Information Age it is gratifying that the English newspapers are written and published at home and are also being printed abroad where required. I can always do without television and - although I thought I'd arranged my broadband connection in France - the Internet but I simply wilt if denied my daily cryptic fix even, as in earlier times, when two days old. The local shop ran out on Saturday and again today and was shut on Sunday. Travelling can be hell ...and Darcey agrees with me.

EU insanity

The English news is reporting that the European

Commission is considering a rule that cars should drive on dipped headlights at all times. This is of course a sensible Scandinavian solution to the short winter days that are a characteristic of the polar regions in which they choose to live. I've noted that irrespective of latitude most drivers already pop their lights on when daytime visibility is poor. Quite how the French, already having quite enough trouble with indicators, will conform to this latest nonsense defeats me.

That's the essential trouble with European government, Arctic Circle solutions to fictional Mediterranean problems.

26th February   'Oh I do like to be beside the seaside.'   Bandol and Sanary sur Mere

La Daby thrives on sunshine. When the sky is blue and the sun is out it has a special uplifting character all its own but when the weather is dull and grey the pine woods become dark and a little menacing and the trees lean downhill, hunching together for support, while glowering down on intruders and their small dogs. Today we have been mutually frowned upon for daring to disturb their peace and duly chastened make plans for a trip to the seaside. Rain or shine I always enjoy the coast; it never fails to remind me of happy childhood family excursions to places like Bognor and Swanage and Sandbanks and their like. Simple youthful pleasures.

Today we shall promenade at nearby literary Bandol, DH Lawrence's erstwhile watering hole. The drive down to the coast gets greyer and more disapproving as the kilometres pass by and we eventually arrive at a damp, rather genteel looking resort where, for today, parking is free as all along the esplanade the weekly Tuesday market is in full flow and thus, in accordance with The Rules, not an inch of parking space, free or otherwise, is to be had.

We progress with due care and attention in a stream of like minded souls along a road lined inland with seaside peddlers' booths and all the cafe culture trappings of a popular resort, and the market on the other - until halted midway by the municipal *gendarmes*. Ahead there is a tangle of rather forlorn vehicles, their emergency indicators flashing, and this muddle is accompanied by impassive policemen in their couture tracksuit uniforms, who get in everybody's way and add to the confusion. Now, it might not have gone unnoticed that I've had a little experience of such matters and Halting Advancing Traffic Approaching From The Front is lesson number one in the traffic cops' handbook, but not here. *Monsieur le flic* merely strolls into the middle of the carriageway, advances on our car and with a frosty stare, defies us to advance another *centimetre*. By the looks of this lean, mean, blue sandpaper jawed minion of the law I'm going nowhere but eventually, one transit van having been extricated, he waves us on with an unexpectedly charming smile and we proceed lawfully on our way.

Truth be told Bandol looks just a little over commercial and over developed for our taste, so we abandon our plans and reverse course but on a whim continue along the coast shortly arriving in Sanary sur Mere. Sanary is smaller, much more to our style and not to be outdone, there's a more manageable market and ready parking space, so we enjoy a leisurely meander and finish with a *café crème* outside a seaside cafe full of traders and their customers.

My wife is from the north-east and in spite of that we love to stay in Northumberland, mostly in and around Budle Bay, Bamburgh, Seahouses and Beadnell and on our travels up and down that coast, with its largely redundant harbours and havens, have often regretted the wreckage that is all that remains of Britain's fishing industry. Working trawlers are few and far between and nowadays our fish is mostly imported, yet here at Sanary, hard by the marina with its yachts and pleasure craft, many small trawlers are tied up alongside and on the quay near their mooring lines, the crews have set up stalls where they sell their catches. We should be doing a lot more to free up our fishermen. One only has to think about Arbroath Smokies and kippers from Craster to know how well we should be doing from our sea girt island.

⌐ ⌐

I love the statuary to be found in French towns and villages. It has style. Occupying the centre of the *place* and competing for room with our cafe and therefore in much danger of being overwhelmed by a multitude of wicker tables and chairs, a slightly eroded renaissance hero gazes blindly seaward from atop his lions' head fountain. Dressed in the ancient Roman manner and boasting an anchor in lieu of a swagger stick, he imperiously introduces the town to the sea, seeking nothing much in return, except perhaps for someone to remove the excessive lengths of copper water spout emerging like unsanitary drinking straws from the lions' mouths and the aluminium fairy light scaffolding

60

entangled like briars about his classical plinth.

After coffee we take to the car and meander further along the seafront road admiring property and comparing prices and views, until the road runs out and we are forced to retrace our steps and return. We have sold up and moved at least twice and admired a social gathering's *al fresco* lunch with wine. A dozen or so folk of a certain age seated together around a table in an almost empty beach car park in a freezing windswept downpour, simply enjoying each other's company. I just can't imagine my wife's church group or the WI, showing equally gritty determination or yet having such an obviously good time.

We dine at home in front of our better behaved log fire on substantial confit duck and sausage cassoulet with dipping chunks of crusty bread, all bought from the local supermarket, and drink a very smooth Côtes du Rhône and all's right with the world.

27th February   Massifs and Monuments   Le Thoronet Abbey

The foresters have been at work in L'Enclos de La Daby this morning and as the drone of their chainsaw echoes around the wood, we are greeted by a large, rough haired, rather proprietorial dog that appears from the trees above our cottage. Even when in the woods I have been careful to demonstrate the best attributes of responsible dog owning by clearing up *après* Darcey but this fellow-me-lad's unsanitary behaviour is obvious and his palpable unconcern leaves much to be desired. Darcey is demure in the presence of this ruffian.

It's a bright warm morning and seizing the moment, we've abandoned inclement weather arrangements for a trip to Marseilles, in favour of an expedition further inland. A boat trip round the harbour to Château D'If with its cast of revolutionary characters will just have to wait.

🐎 🐎

Le Thoronet lies above the Massif Desmaures, which stretches eastwards guarding the coast from the port of Toulon up towards Frejus.

Being English I'd never really considered, much less understood, monasteries until a friend enlightened me. I've been privileged to have had three mentors, all of them army colonels, who encouraged and supported me at different times in my career and Colonel Mike Day, historian and wordsmith *extraordinaire* was the last of my influencers. Catholic gentleman and very much a product of the old school, he was my first boss in business immediately after I had left the army, and so, having tutored me the ways of Mammon, he made amends by introducing me to the various ruins that are Protestant England's remaining contribution to its monastic past.

Relics and excavations and National Trust ground plans are all well and good but as he well knew, they don't give you a feel for the original. Much like Peter Mayle's descriptions of Ménerbes, you don't appreciate the village's height and steepness until you've witnessed it for yourself. Mike's sage advice was to see what the French have done to preserve their abbeys, so we started some years ago at Fontevraud l'Abbaye, Loire monastery and resting place to both English and French royalty.

Today searching the Guide Michelin for an outing, my wife discovered Le Thoronet and while a distant drive, we decide to visit.

Climbing north from Le Beausset we ascend the Massif de la Sainte with its stunning views westward down to La Ciotat on the coast. It's a top down day and the smells of the herbs and pinewoods are a joy. This is a playground and we pass the 'adults only' Paul Ricard motor racing circuit before descending into a valley of camping sites and theme parks for children. I am drawn by a colourful plastic Wild West Indian tented village in the woods and my wife has said that if I'm very, very good...

On through Aubagne, home of the legendary French Foreign Legion, the unmistakably stratified limestone cliffs and woods of the Massif de la Sainte Baume occupies the horizon before us and soon we turn east towards Brignols, where another truly majestic massif, the l'Esterel, stands foursquare in the distance dominating the landscape and shortly we turn north to Carcès and its nearby abbey.

I'd programmed the navigation machine as far as Carcès and much too late we discover that our European Atlas does not condescend to minor roads of the sort that appeal to Cistercian monks or their remote monasteries and my wife has omitted to bring the guide book, which would have at least reminded us of the damn thing's name. As it's in The Rules, the automatic map-reading machine deposits us squarely in the centre of the village where we attempt to dredge up the vocabulary required to enquire after our anonymous abbey. I have a rough idea of the compass bearing, so we pick a road - any road, and after a while just as doubts begin to gnaw, like a drink in the desert, a sign to our bashful destination hoves into view and we turn off.

Le Thoronet Abbey lies in a beautiful mixed landscape of forest and farmland, which manifestly suited the harsh Cistercian way of life. Since its decline Le Thoronet has been declared a site of national importance and thus it is now state owned - consequently bureaucratic lunch is taken between twelve and two. We retire to Carcès to pursue the convention and lunch in a small cafe where we drink a welcome beer and *Madame* serves monumental slabs of lasagne with a delightfully dressed green salad. It's that sort of cafe, where you eat what's been prepared and that's it and all about it!

Later the abbey conforms to pattern. Le Thoronet is a small manageable set of buildings never having supported more than forty odd souls and in the way of many Cistercian communities, its unadorned buildings place worship and hard work side by side.

The abbey church is an austere sanctuary entirely devoid of decoration except where semi circle vaulted side chapels bear faded signs of painted iconography. This was never intended as a place of worship for the laity and consequently there is no central west door and its absence is oddly disturbing.

Le Thoronet's basilica is renowned for its acoustics and whilst exploring I happen across two young folk singers taking advantage of this as they intone haunting, vaguely religious, plainchant while completely alone in this de-consecrated echoing relic.

The French government has had to do a lot to save

64

these buildings as late 20th century mining has destabilized their foundations; on balance it seems a worthwhile way to spend taxpayers' money.

🐕 🐕

Returning home by way of Toulon the motorway is cloudy with mustard coloured mimosa and the air is heady with its scent.

At Toulon, once famously blockaded by Lord Nelson, the *autoroute* does not bypass so much as underpass, circumventing traffic congestion by the simple expedient of burrowing beneath it. This underground motorway is quite the longest road tunnel I've driven and certainly solves the traffic problem. The European Commission should take careful note and perhaps suggest something similar for Sweden. For the sake of clarity I have in mind tunnelling rather than laying siege.

Later we sit outside in the last of the day's warmth and enjoy a lightly chilled bottle of the famed Bandol Rosé, which entirely lives up to its reputation.

28th February   Sightseeing in Le Beausset

Much as in England where the peripatetic first Queen Elizabeth slept about a bit, Napoleon did the same in France and reportedly visited Le Beausset for a month in 1793. After a week here we rather hope that he visited in high season and took in Bandol as well.

We've avoided Le Beausset's old quarter somewhat and in all probability won't be seeking out the equivalent of its 'Napoleon Slept Here' blue plaque in the Rue Louis Pasteur.

Le Beausset Vieux

Out of town however we did take in Le Beausset Vieux which involved driving up the nearby hill where the town's original settlement stood. During the climb I begin to appreciate why the residents opted for life in the valley. The road up the steep sided hill narrows alarmingly and its state of repair does not inspire confidence. Some of the drops, whilst plainly not in the Ardèche Gorge's league, are *interesting* enough to encourage me to select a low gear and take a prudent line.

Thankfully during the climb we avoid meeting opposing traffic and arrive at the hilltop plateau where the view from a small belvedere is incredible. Observe! If it weren't for the murk one could see Marseilles. The drive down is much easier as without one iota of compunction I flock behind another car, which seems to have purpose, or at least knows the way and anyway descending together in line astern we comprise *force majeur.*

29th February   Saint Cyr sur Mere and La Ciotat

Another lovely day, which sees us rising early except for Darcey, who is becoming a real Stop-a-Bed these days.

She's always been a deep sleeper and recently, probably due to her deafness, can be quite difficult to wake. When she first joined the family she was prone to disturbing nightmares. Definitely not the normal eyelid flickering, paw twitching, dead to the world woofing and barking, dreams all dogs enjoy, but the most alarming of episodes from which she would struggle awake groggy, clearly disorientated and often anxious. Similarly once or twice in early days she cowered away from the most innocuous of sudden gestures, wholly innocent on our part. She was also incredibly dependant, a lot more than seemed natural and it took months of very gentle handling to calm her from these maladies. Goodness knows what rotten treatment she had been exposed to before she was abandoned. Nowadays she just takes us for granted which is exactly as it should be.

ㅂ ㅂ

From the din pervading even our small forest glade it is apparent that the local youthful motor bikers are out in force for a Route National burn up and I grumble into my coffee and utter dark threats and imprecations, when it occurs to me that their offensive droning is going on a lot longer that usual. Where are the *gendarme*s when needed? My wife has the answer; it is the nearby Ricard racing circuit warming up for the weekend. Thank goodness we'll be leaving tomorrow before ten.

We decide on a trip along the nearby coast, essentially the shoreline we did not explore earlier in the week. The esplanade roads are quite tight in places and made worse by vans and lorries with essential deliveries and once again I am amazed just how short sighted and mule headed some drivers can be, forcing a way against all comers when the dictates of prudence and common sense and occasionally the rules of the road, would suggest otherwise.

After our morning promenade I was sorely tempted to blacken the characters of the offending French motorists who crossed my path, ready to declare their offending behaviour yet another Gallic vice but I fear it applies everywhere and I only record it here as, unlike them, our journey was largely unnecessary and I was unburdened by urgent business and therefore far less prone to do exactly the same thing myself.

The sea views were worth the trip and it was interesting to see business actually taking place.

This afternoon we will be packing and tidying the cottage as tomorrow morning we take our leave of La Daby and head west into Languedoc-Roussillon for the third of our four cottages.

Chapter Five

Languedoc-Roussillon

The Aude

Languedoc-Roussillon's vineyards were originally created by the Greeks but it was the Romans who shaped the landscape. Significantly their Via Domitia, the southern road running directly from Rome to Spain, was ancient Gaul's oldest thoroughfare and its surviving bridges and *oppida* bear lasting testament to the Roman army's industry and endeavours.

The region's varied landscape of mountains, plains and coast, is rather more unembroidered than Provence but in its own way just as dynamic.

Planted with more than 740 thousand acres of vineyards, this is the world's oldest and largest wine producing area and within this attractive diverse region is to be found the Aude. Situated between the Mediterranean and the Pyrenees this region hosts Carcassonne and many striking villages.

Named for its river and created in Revolutionary times from part of the Languedoc, summer in the Aude is hot dry and windy. Winter is cold and windy whilst short sharp storms are common in the autumn.

The Aude - Vines and olives. Oysters and rugby football. Cassoulet and Cathars.

1st March   Domaine de l'Enclos
Sainte Valière

The dog is in trouble and she knows it, for my wife has expressed displeasure and that means unadulterated, copper-bottomed trouble!   We'd remarked Darcey's increasing age related clinginess and occasionally at home, when we've gone out together leaving her to watch and ward the house, she has expressed canine disapproval by having a grumble. This usually manifests itself by an assault on my walking boots or an out-and-out scrabbling attack on the bedding in her box.   Occasionally on this trip she's been left in the cottage - mainly when we've visited the supermarket and the like since we don't care to leave her in the car - and she's taken to scratching. When I say scratching, she's actually drawn blood from a spot on her offside elbow and she and we, all know that as it never happens at other times, it's sheer bad tempered outrage on her part. We shall have to be firm with her, but even so it's a worrying affair and one that will need careful supervision.   There will be a reckoning, never fear, but for the moment we're going to have to take her everywhere and if that means a sit in *chez* Darcey on the back seat of the car outside the shops, well so be it and one of the party had better start getting used to the idea.

🐕 🐕

We left Le Beausset on schedule and retraced our steps northwards before swinging south-west towards Arles and the Camargue. Thereafter it was a simple drive down to Montpellier and Béziers before turning inland above Narbonne.   My wife has been much more reliable at the tolls, not needing half as much supervision as hitherto and as a result may well be allowed to play with lock gates

70

when we take to the canals for a boat trip later in the week.

The change of scenery was dramatic, driving out of the mountains onto the flat alluvial Camargue was accompanied by strong gusting winds and for a moment we thought that the Mistral was upon us but I think we've been lucky, as things seem to have abated.

Sainte-Valière lies in the heart of Minervois country more or less in the centre of a triangle formed by Béziers, Narbonne and inland, Carcassonne. It is a tiny antique agricultural village where the gated and shuttered, thick walled stone buildings are of an assortment of styles and ages and the village streets meander in a narrow high-sided network around the church and *mairie*. In recent years the village has spread out along its road net as more modern housing as been built but the vineyards still encroach right up to the edges of the village.

Our new cottage is set in the gardens of a large village house now owned by an English couple who reside here. It's a modern addition; one in a block of ten apartments occupying a redundant wine *cave*, purpose built to satisfy the demands of a thriving holiday business.

2nd March   Domaine de l'Enclos

We awake late regretting not having gate-crashed the next-door apartment's party that went on a bit last night. It's a beautiful bright morning and the wind has died down so Darcey and I head for the vineyard for a constitutional and *en route* meet our host. He is a guitar playing carpenter from the south of London who fled England years ago and clearly in love with this bit of France, is now domiciled here.   We talk as men do, of wine, and rugby, the price of property and cirrhosis of the liver.

En vignes the air is clear and in the distance way to the south the peaks of the Pyrenees are snow covered.   We trudge on through the serried ranks of vines and as we go admire here and criticise there, as if we actually knew what we were talking about.   The dog adores it, as do I.

Situated just so as to spoil the view and compete with the electricity pylons, the local authorities have planted thickets of electricity generating wind turbines.   From our vineyard two rather attractive nearby heights are blighted by these monstrous machines, semaphoring by day and flashing Morse code from anti-collision strobe lights by night and I wonder who it is that they are signalling and what their lunatic message can possibly be?

We return to Domaine de l'Enclos where I let the dog off her lead and she promptly heads off following an arbitrary right angle to investigate significant canine matters while I skirt the pool and head towards our cottage.   After a long moment or two we find ourselves at opposite sides of the swimming pool and Darcey, suddenly discovering that my interest in her olfactory affairs is at best lukewarm and that she has become detached, peers about in her myopia to find me.   Over time I've come to realize that she has more of a chance spotting movement and not pausing to consider the swimming pool lying between us, wave my arms and call out to her.   It is immediately obvious that the dog is comforted to be reunited with her family so, head up and tail wagging and completely ignoring the intervening water obstacle, she sets off to rejoin us.

With much effort from all concerned we avoid hateful water, unintentional doggie paddling and consequent rescues.

More seaside adventures

The top's down and we are on pilgrimage. When last in France we stayed near Perpignan and spent a memorable lazy afternoon at Narbonne Plage. This seaside resort is about fifteen kilometres from Narbonne itself and we decide to revisit. Darcey and her house are loaded into the back and we enjoy a pleasant morning's drive over.

I've been a fierce critic of our home town's Burghers as they have, in my view, been derelict in repairing the roads, which are consequently awash with potholes. In the light of recent experience I take it all back; I am remiss; I retract; manfully, I apologise. They are not the worst in the world for, unquestionably, their French cousins are of inferior stock, beating them all hands down. In fact they make our bunglers look positively amateur. Not only are French minor roads hereabouts in an appalling condition but their awfulness has been improved with traffic calming speed bumps. Fair's fair, it must be acknowledged that such measures occasionally have merit, especially when placed in the vicinity of schools but these sleeping *gendarme*s are, without doubt, the most fearsome suspension wrecking devices known to man. Positioned with missionary zeal to trap unsuspecting heretics and compete with bottomless sunken drains, not only are they endowed with slopes of a height and gradient to shame the Great North-East Ridge of Everest but sometimes they are decorated with painted triangles to warn the unwary and occasionally not. Traffic calming as an oxymoron springs to mind.

On arrival at Narbonne Plage we take a *café crème* in a seafront restaurant, which, whilst delicious, costs approximately twice the National Debt. I'm disappointed but take comfort in the fact the VAT will probably enable the good Burghers of Narbonne to construct another road bump somewhere.

Later this afternoon we relaxed in the sun with a glass of local Minervois and Darcey and I undertook another circuit of our vineyard. The dog has not scratched at all, all day - I knew it was just wrath, the little swine.

3rd March   Domaine de l'Enclos
Ste Valière in Perspective

Darcey and I are just back from our morning vineyard stroll and we've been reflecting on disorder; well not quite disorder more an untidiness, a certain lack of symmetry. It starts with the apartment, which is built in an old wine *cave*. We've noticed that nothing is quite in true. No doubt accommodating the original layout and structure, the rooms are just not square and, as my wife observes, the perspective is wrong and this is improved by a certain minimalist look, which all rather adds to the charm.

In the fields outside the village I am disturbed, albeit in a minor key, by the numerous wind turbines, which almost fail to dominate the landscape hereabouts. I don't doubt their green credentials but I do rather quail at their half-baked intrusiveness and somewhat chaotic demeanour. They are simply untidy and rather graceless.

At first flush there is a regularity as they are uniformly stark white and, allowing for the laws of perspective, the same size but there things end.   Ranked on high ground their dressing is wrong as, probably due to the nature of the terrain they occupy, the distance between them varies in both alignment and depth. Frankly they are an untidy muddle and this is not helped by their unsynchronized blades, which sail silently round at different speeds. Like an ungainly squad of new recruits they lack coordination and demonstrate great difficulty in Saluting to the Front. While we walk they hove into view then slide away in parallax, as though appearing for the press and then sneaking away so as to avoid the question. High off to the east silhouetted darkly against the morning sun, a particularly odious gaggle are vaguely reminiscent of a modern Calvary except there are far too many thieves. It's all rather offensive to my tidy soldier's eye.

It's only much later that I discover that the Aude's characteristic winds are the reason these farms are positioned hereabouts and that a village restaurant is called Les Treize Vents (*Thirteen Winds*) in celebration of them.

꒲ ꒱

The weather is verging on the stay at home variety and after some debate we decide to drive to Carcassonne to seek a newspaper and an English language tourist's guide as we wish to explore some of the Cathar castles that lurk nearby. In the event this turns out to be a fool's errand so we turn for home on the promise of a good lunch to make up for it. After discovering that everywhere we pause is closed we end up almost back where we started within two kilometres of Ste Valière in a tucked away roadside *auberge*.

We start with a Caesar salad, which, like most Caesar salads I choose lately, isn't. This *entrée* comprises a nicely dressed green salad and lacking shaved parmesan, offers instead a topping of super thin escallop of breaded chicken - together with a stuffed roast tomato, one lone anchovy and just a hint of grated cheese. Whatever this dish was, it was *not* a classic Caesar salad but as salad starters go it was a rather good, if somewhat out of the ordinary, combination. My wife ordered grilled chicken while I opted for a sensible assembly of pork and mushrooms. Her chicken was accompanied by unexpected *frites*. These arrived slightly late but in much style, wrapped in an individual paper cone that was in turn embraced within the ornamental twists of a chrome plated apparatus - designed solely and wholly to hold paper cones of potato chips - which, oh joy, included a compartment dedicated to dipping mayonnaise. This culinary lunacy unquestionably made up for all the morning's disappointments.

After lunch we discover an English Michelin Guide in our local supermarket, which my wife had obviously failed to spot when we looked for it on Saturday. We shall try harder tomorrow.

4th March   Castles at Carcassonne

It has rained overnight - would that one could write that as worthy of note in England. Not only has it rained but there's a cold wind. Very cold! The dog and I inspect our now muddy vineyard at a trot and rush back to the cottage for morning tea and toast. In our absence the local Michelin Guide has been consulted but this version is less than adequate in its description of the castles we'd like to visit, which is quite odd as the Guide is normally right on the button. We decide to return to Carcassonne and visit the medieval city.

I like canals. The calm appeals and I love their unruffled tranquillity and the ducks. The Canal du Midi meanders unhurriedly along empty just now but full of promise for the summer.

The drive over is gusty. Although the avenues of plane trees that trace the canal's path are still bare of leaves and largely unaffected, their coniferous cousins bend and sway in the breeze. We cross and recross the canal and not being of the canal building fraternity and thus ignorant of the finer points of waterway construction, are surprised when at one point the industrious French Navigators had seen fit to construct a canal mooring basin some feet above the river Aude. Later my wife discovers that the canal is planted with shade trees to prevent the water evaporating in the fierce summer heat.

Originally fortified by the Romans, Carcassonne stands foursquare between the Pyrenees and the Massif Central covering ancient trade routes. Its defences were built to dominate this valley and the lie of the land clearly demonstrates its builders' intent.

I'm told that the old city is one of France's most visited attractions and in some respects we're lucky to be here in low season as even with the foul weather we've brought along for the ride, it's fairly busy.   I'm grateful that here at least the Burghers of Carcassonne, unlike their dilatory counterparts at Avignon, have managed to organise adequate car parking facilities.

Carcassonne's old city is an original, largely authentic, medieval township.   Fortunately rescued from 19th century demolition and restored, it is set high above the valley and still occupied.   Although almost certainly bogus afterthoughts, its turrets and tiles bestow it with an enchanted feel - it's a Camelot of a place, almost Disney but without Tinkerbelle and just a touch of the trademark Gibbs Toothpowder castle thrown in for compensation.

We breach the defences through the gates and ramparts of the Porte Narbonnaise, crossing a dry moat by way of a portcullis guarded drawbridge, until a final arched gateway, set between massive twin towers, admits us to the medieval town.   Here shops and houses lean together above the narrow street and snake and jostle upward before us leading towards the castle keep and its formidable barbican.

The craft guilds and traders of old are now entirely replaced with droll tourist shops and their identical plastic products but it is here among the tinsel that my wife eventually spots our still needed catalogue of Cathar castles. Cobbled streets rise steeply to the palace citadel where we turn aside to the Romanesque cathedral of St Nazaire et St Celese and above our heads, incredible carved stone gargoyles leap from its walls to frighten the ungodly while baptising them with surplus rain water. Hard nearby an exclusive hotel breaths wealth and prosperity at us but being insufficiently rich, we scurry away to find a more day-tripper friendly business to sell us a restorative and sorely needed, *café crème* - this time at just a little less than twice the National Debt.

We have thoroughly enjoyed our visit and irrespective of the weather, regret not having spent longer here. For a moment or two during our icy tramp back to the car we envy the few remaining residents their fashionable address. But soon a colder reality takes hold and our covetousness wanes as we begin to appreciate that the people here are trapped on the horns of a curious dilemma. The citizens of this fairytale city are under constant siege, not as in earlier times from infidels and invaders, but from ever present crowds of intrusive tourists on whom, in the long run, they are utterly dependent. It's an odd thought, one that will remain, and it takes me back to semi-retired military friends, Yeoman Warders at the Tower of London, who had similar tales to tell, but they at least, courtesy of the Guards Division, could lock the gates at night and sleep sound in their beds.

Returning to Ste Valière the weather turns dark and cold and wet so we retire to the relative warmth of our cottage and irrespective of such minor setbacks open a rather acceptable bottle of Minervois and contemplate selling up and moving to France. I persuade my wife that *cassoulet* would be most acceptable for supper, which only adds to my determination.

5th March   Domaine de l'Enclos
Ste Valière

It's stopped raining and the sky is bright but a brutal

cold wind turns our morning constitutional into something of a gallop. At least the wind has dried off the surface mud in the vineyards.

Whilst it's not raining cats and dogs we do see evidence of the local fauna. A great ginger Bagpuss of a cat lies in a sandbagged heap in a garage door sun trap and is entirely unconcerned by our passing. Its next-door neighbour is an uncouth bruiser of a dog, which tries every device known to dogdom to force its nose legs and body beneath its substantial garden gate intent on savaging first Darcey and then me. It howls and bays and sobs in frustration throwing itself into the gap until well after we are out of range when it promptly directs its attention to the next innocent victim.

There is a stand of tall woolly, rather dense pines in a garden near the vineyard and the trees are absolutely full of birds. Even though I'm as deaf as a post I can hear them twittering and chirping.

Not uncommonly among soldiers of my generation, I suffer gunfire-induced tinnitus and deafness, fondly known as Gunner Ear - a description that alone can cause certain amusement among the uninitiated, especially during noisy cocktail parties - and this damage effectively ended my ambition to fly army helicopters. In my day, before being accepted for flying training, pilot candidates had to undergo various intellectual and physical tests together with a comprehensive medical examination, all courtesy of the Royal Air Force.

Having adequately demonstrated that I could add and subtract, the junior service determined that I could coordinate my eyes and hands, measured my limbs and agreed that I could fit in an aircraft and see beyond the end of my nose. Then came the hearing tests. Fitted with headphones I was, ear by ear, to record the number of BBC pips of diminishing volume and increasing frequency that I could detect. Well, in the upper registers all this candidate could hear was the usual ringing in his head. One can bluff one's way only so far and my limitations discovered, a Very Senior RAF Medical Type declared: 'Now young man, you don't seem to hear so well.' In vaguely rhetorical manner: 'Pardon?' I rejoined. Sighing a very superior sigh and demonstrating much restraint, the Very Senior Medical Type asked when last I'd heard the dawn chorus. All indecision I paused and, observing my uncertainty, the Senior Medical Type softened - charitably explaining that: 'It's not that it's not happening. It's just that you can't hear it!' We agreed that I would remain land-borne.

In their trees the birds squabble and chatter and haggle for better perches but for all that remain invisible.

5th March   Minerve
Les Plus Beaux Villages de France [2]

1210 AD was not a bad year for Simon de Montfort as following his successful earlier investment of Carcassonne, he laid siege to and eventually wrested the castle of Minerve from its hereditary lords. After massacres in Beziers a group of Cathars had sought refuge in the village and de Monfort's six-week attack on the

---

[2] 'The Most Beautiful Villages of France' Award Scheme.

81

fortifications and water supply resulted in comprehensive destruction and the surrender of the defenders.

Traditionally the capital of the Minervois wine region, the village and the surviving remnants of its battered fortress lie atop a steep sided gorge of the river Cesse to the north-west of St Valière and the drive out is a pleasant combination of vineyards and rocky hills.

Towards and about the village the ravines are sheer and the views spectacular that is until one remembers that this landscape bore witness to the surrender of Guillaume de Minerve on condition that the lives of his defeated followers be spared. The gentlemen's agreement stood until the victors invited the defeated heretics to recant and the 140 or so who declined to oblige were promptly burned at the stake.

Later we drive to Béziers and on the way once again discuss houses and moving here to live and my wife falls in love with a far off turreted hilltop residence of some style. We agree that once we win the National Lottery it will be hers and think no more about it.

Oppidum

Returning by a different route we make our way to Ensérune a wonderful ancient high point inhabited from the Bronze Age but abandoned in the late Roman era. The hilltop has been partly excavated and its Roman town exposed and investigated, and having wended our way aloft discover that the site's Museum is the very building my wife has set her heart upon.

We park and climb the final 100 feet or so up to the

site via a steep rustic stairway and both Darcey and I, being of a certain age and disposition, have difficulties with the inconsistency of the steps and in negotiating the higher risers. My knees creak and the dog succeeds only after two falls and a submission.

Arriving at the top the gardens are spectacular with gorgeous views of the Aude valley and the Canal du Midi winding along below. The north wind, which has been against us all day, is fierce here but the southern aspects are sheltered and remarkably warm. One can quite see why the site attracted occupation but not why it subsequently fell into disuse.

To the north lies the drained Montady Lake; a prominent landscape feature with its star shaped drainage system dating from the 13th century. Viewed from above it is remarkably akin to a massive fertile darts board in the landscape - with the pretty village of Montady occupying the double eighteen slot.

6th March   Domaine de l'Enclos
Ste Valière   Narbonne

The cold north wind that has been plaguing us since we arrived here shows absolutely no signs of abating. When my wife spoke on the telephone to our hosts before leaving for France they boasted of lunching on the patio and half in jest, I said that with our luck we'd probably arrive with the Mistral in tow. Now we're here, I'm expected to take seriously the claim that it just doesn't reach these parts and that's as maybe, but the freezing gale force winds that are almost blowing Darcey's ears off seem to be putting up a pretty good imitation.

83

Even though the weather is bright and clear and in occasional suntraps pleasantly warm, the storm force winds makes sightseeing distinctly uncomfortable and as a result we spend the late morning in the local area house viewing from the car before driving over to the coast to allow Narbonne Plage a second chance. We've already seen a number of village locations that appeal, mostly round the Canal du Midi and our host's son, who is involved in a local construction business, has kindly been a mine of information.

After a gentle drive through the rather attractive rocky hinterland we arrive more or less in time for a late lunch and, while the car is sand blasted in the esplanade car park, indulge in a very tasty light lunch of pasta in a beach side restaurant.

We conclude that property here is far too Popular Holiday Resort in shades of pastel for our taste, being moribund in winter, insufferably energetic in summer and unbearably colourful throughout. Much like living with the Ovaltinies - happy girls and boys!

Road improvements?

Driving home we are unwilling witnesses to the death of two miles of mature roadside trees sacrificed at the altar of road improvements. Since the existing road seemed more than adequate I'm tempted to despair but it's not my country, I don't pay taxes here and it's none of my damn business; but I regret it nonetheless.

Traffic

In Narbonne I'm reminded of the dangers associated with some urban traffic lights, which change instantly from red to green with no amber, sequence in between. Under this system where traffic is liable to congestion, Red Light Jumpers are prone to cause absolute bedlam without any option to become an Amber Gambler, which at least buys a little time and distance.   Oh joy. Oh bliss. Oh poop-poop!

Later the navigating machine leads us a merry dance on back roads and tracks during which we discover that, again contrary to popular belief, French drivers do give way and do acknowledge politeness but, and it must be said, I have been sorely tempted to pull up on the carriageway to invite younger French drivers to view the contents of my car's boot - rather than allow them to attempt a close inspection at 50mph whilst chatting on their mobile phones.

Manners

Yet again I am impressed by the politeness exhibited by one and all in France. Everyone I meet greets me with a *'Bonjour'* or whatever is appropriate for the time of day and even the schoolchildren who I pass on my morning walks with Darcey hereabouts, speak politely.   In the shops and restaurants expressions of greeting and thanks are commonplace and clearly genuine sentiments; unlike the habitual 'Have a nice day' now intoned throughout Britain as meaningless ritual in the observance of Quality and Customer Service.

Coffee

At home in England it's my wife who is the coffee drinker but when abroad I tend to join her addiction. It strikes us both that, starting on board the Sea France ferry, wherever we go in this country we've never had a poor or indifferent cup of coffee. Would that you could make the same claim for the UK.

7th March   Domaine de l'Enclos

It's Friday and it's getting colder and darker by the hour but the optimists among us have foretold better weather for the weekend. Since we've not had the papers or television for the best part of a week, I strongly suspect someone's been at the tea leaves. Anyway we leave for Bordeaux tomorrow.

On the way to our vineyard I was interested to see a dozen or so trophy pigs' trotters nailed in untidy display to one of the large double wooden gates that commonly face the streets in French villages. Hairy and blackened with age I imagine they are from wild *sanglier* and exhibited much the way that I've seen vicious freshwater Pikes' heads fastened above barn doors in England. It rather brings home the fact that quite wild country lies not too far away in and around this Aude valley. I later discover that this is Peter the Hunter's house and the trotters are indeed the spoils of successful hunting expeditions in the nearby hillside woods. Our Host confirms that there is much game hereabouts and that the local vineyards are the roost of pheasants but I found that at this time of year there is insufficient cover and thus not much evidence of them.

Marketing - Aude style

All week on our way back through the vineyard I've been pondering the village church's clock tower. Prominent above the rooftops it's topped by an unusual metal openwork construction. In the normal manner of most church steeples and towers, Ste Valière's church is possessed of a very fine weathervane with a magnificently patriotic tricolour weathercock to gauge the wind. Set slightly below, the church also boasts four prominent somewhat old-fashioned loudspeakers rather akin to those to be found on Islamic minarets.

Hitherto mute, these less than commonplace artefacts usually serve to indicate the cardinal points of the compass but this morning mid vineyard, they buzzed and crackled into life at 9:25 precisely. To the merry accompaniment of ice cream van chimes, rather than calling the faithful to prayer, they grandly announced to the empty countryside and those citizens still abed, that the mobile butcher and baker had arrived in town. This I think demonstrates that the entrepreneurial qualities of the Roman Catholic Church are still alive and of a very high order indeed. God and Mammon working together for the good of the community; a PR man's dream come true. Mind you with its hollow railway concourse echoes and the volume set to rattle glass I'd have hated to be beset with a hangover at the time.

Our host later tells me that hereabouts such methods of village communication are not as uncommon as I had at first supposed and can at times be a bit of a nuisance. I'm of the opinion that a town crier has much more style if rather less carrying power.

Later we drive south to visit the Abbey de Fontfroide and too late discover the detour home that we should have taken yesterday having paid far too much attention to the GPS, which we have found tends to lie like a cheap NAAFI watch unless closely minded.

Like most Abbeys the privately owned Abbey de Fontfroide with its much-admired collection of roses is set in idyllic countryside and although its grounds are open the Abbey buildings seem only available by tour and resist our attempts to find a way in. So like the heretics of Minerve we decline and instead of the stake the weather worsens in disapproval as we wend our way home.

Founded in 1093 AD the Abbey Sainte-Marie de Fontfroide achieved status and prominence during Pope Innocent III's campaign against the Cathar heretics but like many others was dissolved during the French Revolution. Later refounded and yet again deconsecrated we discover that the Abbey was privately purchased in the early 20th century by the artists Gustave and Madeleine Fayet d'Andoque to protect its fabric.

It's our last day here and so there will be inevitable administration connected with moving on. My wife is officer-in-charge of moving on and I find it prudent to remember that at all times. Our hosts have invited us for drinks this evening and that will be nice.

Chapter Six

Aquitaine

Roman Gallia Aquitania bounded in the south by Spain and the east by the Midi-Pyrenees, Aquitaine faces west to the Atlantic and is a green rolling landscape where the confluence of the rivers Garonne and Dordogne form the vast Gironde estuary.

Conquered by the Romans, lost to the Visigoths, incorporated into the Frankish kingdom and created a duchy in the 9th century, this whole region was in the possession of the English until lost to France by poor bewildered Henry VI in 1453.

Named for its dukes and homeland of the romantic, renowned and imprisoned Queen Eleanor (*of whom more later*) wife of Louis VII and later Henry II of England and mother of Richard the Lionheart, it largely comprises Gascony a land historically inhabited by the Basques.

With its many medieval townships and villages containing the cities and towns of Bordeaux, Bayonne Biarritz and Bergerac, Aquitaine is famous for its oysters, geese, *paté*, truffles and claret.

Le pays d'Aquitaine - home of d'Artagnan of *The Three Musketeers*, food, *foie gras,* Armagnac and *douceur de vivre*!

9th March   Rose Cottage   Listrac Gironde

Yesterday morning we left Ste Valière still in the throes of wind and worsening weather. Apart from the conditions our stay had been very pleasant and we agree that we would certainly visit there again. Before we left the owners gave a small drinks party to which we were invited and they and their guests were most helpful with many tips and advice on moving to France. We'd like to think our next stay will be en route to a new property as we take up residence later in the year.

Even in my delicate condition we got away on time and the four-hour drive to Bordeaux and our new cottage took us up the Aude valley and via Toulouse into Aquitaine.

Toulouse has a very Silicon Valley feel and trades on Aerospace which it has been doing since Concorde was jointly built here in the 1960s. We were interested to pass a decommissioned Arianne rocket ready to launch from a nearby business park just to reinforce the point.

The *autoroute* climbs high up into the Midi Pyrenees before descending following the Garrone River through Agen towards the Atlantic. The changing landscape becomes more agricultural and lush as we climb and the viniculture gives way to a mixed farming regime before intensifying again lower down on the far slopes.

This is our fourth and last week's stay in France and we are lodging in a cottage a little above the famed wine centre of St Émilion. The Vines and Roses cottages are adjuncts of a small but rather stylish *chateau* tucked for protection in a pretty fold.

The vineyards here have a much different character. At this time of year under the Atlantic maritime influence the fields are lush and surrounded with largely deciduous trees. Apart from the nature of the buildings there is a very English feel and when Darcey and I inspect our new territory we notice the catkins bursting forth and there is heavy dew on the grass so we return to the cottage with six wet feet.

The vines in our immediate neighbourhood have a quite sophisticated feel. I suspect that it's to do with the fact that the fields are underplanted with grass rather than the more rugged rubble littered bare soil in the Aude and Rhône and they command the greensward in blocks – a bit like formed Napoleonic infantry waiting to receive cavalry.

Apart from the usual routine of re establishing ourselves in a new location, which to be honest is now more or less routine, we've not decided on a programme for this week but there are one or two matters to be attended to. We must book Logis accommodation for the journey back to Calais and organise the Sea France sailing. We have been toying with a fifth week's stay in the Loire but Easter, early this year, is on the horizon and we decide to return before the school holidays make travelling a little more difficult. Thankfully there's a cyber cafe in St Émilion as the arrangements with my mobile phone and the laptop are laboured to the point of inertia.

10th March Rose Cottage

It's Monday and it's raining and blowing and it rained

yesterday, all things considered not a very auspicious start to our Aquitaine visit. In the wet Darcey and I managed a couple of constitutionals around our new vineyard but the balance of the party decided that a day indoors was probably a good idea and having towelled dry the remainder quickly agreed with the proposal.

The entrance to our cottage is up a short flight of expanded metal steps and while Darcey can get down them well enough, going up is a more sedate matter with some fumbling as she seeks to Spot The Steps before ascending. However, once she's on the first tread we're off to the races and as I lifted her up this morning I was strongly reminded of our first encounter.

That year we had moved north for business, occupying a new house with all that entails. Our previous dog, an attractive but noisy rescued black Whipadore (or *possibly a Labret, we were never quite sure*) having suffered chronic kidney failure in the summer, Christmas celebrations without a dog on the mat were likely to have a hole in their heart.   One Sunday morning in early December I was fulfilling a duty by writing to my brother in New Zealand and this infrequent and erratic activity was accompanied by all sorts of delicious smells emanating from the kitchen where festive culinary preparations were in full swing. Consequently I just happened to reflect that Christmas would be just a little hollow that year there being no dog supervising preparations in the kitchen.   Now, it is my wife's custom to add a line or two and reading what I'd written mused that she missed the dog as well. Spotting the opening…!

The Dog's Home, found just off a major arterial road, is a smart, clean but rather institutional affair, comprising lodgings for boarders and accommodation for strays and is staffed by capable young kennel maids. We arrive and having declared our interest, are shown to The Strays' Kennels, where, in a block vaguely reminiscent of a canine Alcatraz, the recalcitrant and wayward mongrels of Manchester are temporarily housed. We inspect the stock and two to a cell the rebellious hooligans howl and snarl and when not circling with intent, hurl themselves at the wire doors in a frustration of rage. We are alarmed - this is not quite what we had in mind at all. Bravely we continue along until in the penultimate kennel, a small white hangdog is discovered sitting on a mat - her frown and quivering bottom lip clearly advertising that she really does not know: 'Why I am here among these louts?'

My wife immediately goes On Point clearly recognising a kindred spirit. Could this be a Jack Russell terrier of similar ilk to my parents' Jack Russell who adopted my wife at an early age? But yes! Well - maybe?

The dog is inspected, interrogated and after a largish bail has been posted, she is released from custody into our care on probation. Subsequently we Probationers accompany Madam to the car where I insist absolutely, utterly, definitely, that the dog will travel in the foot well. My wife agrees, albeit with what I later came to recognise as A Knowing Smile and whilst I hold open her door and untangle the dog, by now thoroughly knotted in her lead, my wife enters the car and occupies the front passenger seat. The dog, by now unfettered and feigning inexperience, graciously accepts my assistance to enter next and I lift her into her place to settle at my wife's feet. The passenger door slams shut and by the time I have circled the car, entered, and occupied the driver's seat, she is to be found, not in her assigned position but on my wife's lap clinging desperately to her chest and showing absolutely no intention of letting go. This is one of those 'Please Don't Send Me Back To Jail' moments and in the face of mutiny among *all* the crew I relent.

She's a pretty animal, typical of the breed but overlarge with endearingly big feet and thankfully without some of the usual Jack Russell vices, and reaching home she bustles about ensuring that things are just so and generally taking charge. She should be named and what with the short legs and bustling becomes Darcey Bussell forthwith. I'm sure that the lovely ballerina of the same name but infinitely longer legs and much more poise, would not have demurred for a moment.

🐕 🐕

The Vines and Roses cottages are recent and very attractive conversions occupying the rear of the *château's* wine *cave*, which considering our recent addresses would appear to be the fashion, although I am cheered that a certain amount of this building's earlier use has been retained. The original *cave* is tiled in the Romanesque fashion and built of the rubble and stone clunch construction commonly found in France. The windows and doors have been finished like the main house, in a lovely dressed honey grey stone and their fittings completed in a pale tanned wood. Within, the feel of space and light has been retained and a smart en suite bedroom created through the erection of a gallows like platform floor except that the contorted original oak roof supports are too low for a hanging and someone's forgotten the trap.

Altogether it's a sensitive and pleasing alteration and together with the welcoming committee and provisions, which included the local St Émilion wine, bodes well for the week, rain notwithstanding.

We have friends who live in the Canary Isles where they run a successful swimming pool maintenance company. Now, I'm a student of business but I confess that, until we arrived here, I'd never given a great deal of thought to the process or methods they employ... Lurking in the courtyard I discover a rain swept pair of *hommes* who are engaged in stripping the protective cover from the pool. Now you do not need a business degree to realize that in a gale, a winter's worth of accumulated waste and leaf mould might have other intentions than amiable inertia and I wonder if they intend to sweep the yard before attempting alchemy. When we return the technicians have departed and the hitherto clear pool is awash with debris. Perhaps that's how you're supposed to do it?

Politics 'You can't teach an old dogma new tricks.'

Dorothy Parker

In quiet periods, mostly when driving in the car, discussions and plans are moving ahead for our permanent move to France and during a recent conversation we fell to considering the attraction. We both felt that apart from the obvious lures, a significant contributory factor was a shared desire to get away from

England. Better weather and a Mediterranean life style are influential rewards but to be honest we feel rather detached from and disappointed by, the way today's Britain is developing. Of whatever complexion the political system seems weighted in favour of the idle and shiftless and is manned but certainly not managed, by trimmers and the avaricious who generally lack the courage of their convictions. Most legislation seems arbitrary and eye catching rather than considered and well thought through and we are much concerned about the greater than ever erosion of citizens' rights. Over-burdensome taxation and soaring inflation are worrying ...and the police are getting younger!

We know that things might not be much better abroad but at least we'll have voted with our feet and won't be expected to voice an opinion. Lord! How I hate politicians. It's such a shame that no one will ever ask why we're moving, much less care.

ಸ್ಥ ಸ್ಥ

It continues miserable and rather than remain trapped indoors we took a drive into St Émilion but it was so dismal that exploring on foot would have been wretched so we drove on towards Bordeaux, eventually arriving at Libourne which was worse and so cut our losses and limited ourselves to a quick shop. Just to celebrate the event my poor wife trapped her finger in the car door when the wind blew it shut. She has been very brave, much more than I would have been in the circumstances, and the offending digit has now turned a deep blue with purple highlights.

Later we lunched at the cottage and have been making

contingency plans to cut our losses and return home if the weather doesn't improve in short order. Unfortunately Britain is suffering stormy weather and it might be difficult to get a sailing so we may be forced to stay. We shall just have to pray for improved weather if for no other reason than this diary will become mind-numbingly tedious if confined to the 'Wet again – read!' genre.

11th March   Rose Cottage

Rain again; dismal penetrating cold rain. Are we happy? No we're not! On the other hand we've had a couple of unexpected telephone sessions with friends calling which was rather agreeable. I suspect that they think we've gone native but we've shared gossip and they all seem pleased that we've had such an enjoyable time.

Today we shall be making a few calls ourselves as we take time to organize homeward travel arrangements and the hope is that the filthy weather abates so that we'll be able to sail to the UK early next week as planned. Just now we're hanging on to every available weather forecast and this has merely served to highlight how inadequate and incomprehensible most of them actually are. We're becoming quite critical and not a little frustrated, as a succession of pretty presenters, of several genders, wave their arms, press buttons and prattle mysterious incantations. To a man or woman, they fill their allotted time with staccato, almost intelligible, O level data while a dull background with bright intervals dips and wheels dizzily behind them. It's quite a show unless that is you actually want to know what the weather is likely to be!

The pool chap has returned and this morning is

engaged in sub aqua vacuuming. I affect interest and attempt to keep my face straight.

11th March   Rose Cottage   Later

Enough is enough! Outside the driving rain is now horizontal and even if the weather abates over the next few days we're already sodden and fed up and have therefore decided to head for home and be damp in a little more comfort.

We intend to journey north through the Loire and Normandy and since the route is just a little far to drive in one stage my wife is currently booking hotels with the ever-superb Logis de France. Sea France seems to have gone on strike without consulting us so we'll fly the flag and sail back to Dover on the slightly more expensive P&O Ferries. I've announced our intentions to the housekeeper and after putting her mind at ease regarding our motives, we agree that there are only so many wet vineyards that can be viewed before one's enthusiasm wanes. She confirmed that the local weather forecast is not good for the remainder of the week so I think we've made the correct decision.

As usual we'll try to get away by about 10:00 am and then drive north along the Atlantic coast for an overnight pause at Chinon in the Loire. Chinon, where according to legend Joan of Arc encountered and identified the incognito Dauphin, is another of those quaint medieval townships, which abound in France. We stayed nearby some years ago and have been wedded to its wine ever since, tending to enjoy it as a treat with our Christmas goose. Since we should arrive by early afternoon I'd like to take the opportunity to make a return visit to Fontevraud l'Abbaye to inspect the restoration progress we last saw in the 1980s. The following day we'll trek north-east through Normandy's hinterland for an overnight stay near St Omer before heading for the ferry early on Friday morning.

It's a shame to leave earlier than planned but the weather is unpleasant and unlikely to improve before our original departure date. Even sightseeing from the car is difficult in the blustery wet conditions and manifestly unfair on other workaday traffic.

Chapter Seven

Homeward Bound

'Homeward bound,
I wish I was,
Homeward bound,
Home where my thought's escaping…'

Paul Simon

The Loire

12th March Chinon and Fontevraud-l'Abbaye

The four-hour drive up to Chinon from the Gironde was dull. After careful consideration I have to admit that dull is far too feeble a word to describe the exquisite tediousness of the drive which, for the most part was uphill, windy and wet.

Our latest stop made up for it. After a couple of false starts we discovered Le Haut Clos tucked up on a steep wooded hillside above the Vienne River albeit on Chinon's unfashionable left bank. Our new Logis hotel has a comfortable ambience just the better side of shabby, which seems to me entirely appropriate.

Fontevraud - l'Abbaye

Before booking-in we take the opportunity to detour about 15km west to revisit Fontevraud-l'Abbaye and check on developments. We last saw the Royal Abbey some twenty years ago, when construction and restoration, particularly in the Abbey church, was still in progress.

The Royal Abbey of Fontevraud lies to the south of the Loire valley between Saumur and Tours just above Candes Saint Martin and Montsoreu where the Vienne flows into the Loire.

We arrive in the early afternoon, convenient parking is immediately available and while not having the grounds and buildings entirely to ourselves, the Abbey is pleasantly quiet.

Originally a Benedictine monastery and later a convent it was founded in 1101 AD and boasted a number of royal and noble ladies among its thirty-six abbesses before it was closed and converted into a prison in the late Napoleonic period. That drastic conversion and subsequent neglect had a hugely detrimental effect on the buildings' fabric, which only started to be repaired and put to rights in the early 20th century, and remedial work continues to this day.

The Abbey church - a masterpiece in pale honey stone - is regarded as an English royal shrine since four Plantagenet kings and queens were buried here. The remarkably well preserved coloured stone and wood tomb effigies of Henry II and his wife Eleanor of Aquitaine, together with their son Richard I, *Coeur de Lion,* and daughter-in-law Isabelle of Angoulême, the wife of Robin Hood's wicked King John Lackland, lie prominently at peace in the echoing nave and are lit high from above by a luminous stained glass window with the armorial Lions of England glowing in its centre. It is unfortunate that the actual graves were ransacked and lost in Revolutionary times but regardless an unknown benefactor has placed a single remembrance rose beside Queen Eleanor's effigy.

When last we visited here the statues lay in the dusty midst of something akin to a particularly down at heel builder's yard; more generously an indoor archaeological dig. Now the figures lay crowned and caparisoned, held tight in their medieval cots, fittingly restored and raised up on polished beige marble. In death with the ladies on the gentlemen's right, Queen Eleanor reads in bed, doubtless a religious tract, while alongside, her penitent husband, still remorseful for the murder of his friend, Archbishop Thomas à Becket, presents arms with a disappointing sceptre. At their feet the martial Lionheart is surprisingly defenceless having misplaced his sword but his wooden sister-in-law Isabelle lies in state beside him to make up for it.

Outside in the sun dappled Cloisters we visit the *calefactory*; in its day the convent's single heated room from which the poor nuns could benefit and in which perform needlework, and on a nearby wall, a rogues' gallery of the Abbesses complete with photo ID, signet seals and coats of arms is prominently displayed.

Further along in the Chapter House, idealized frescoes representing scenes from the life of Christ are rendered in a primitive style and are somewhat improved with the inclusion of some of the more celebrated religious ladies. Veiled in deepest mourning black with implausible wimples they assume suitably pious poses as befitting late additions to Christ's Passion and Resurrection.

On a more sombre note we pass a memorial tablet commemorating fourteen people executed here and in concentration camps by the Nazis when the Abbey was used to hold members of the French Resistance during the war.

Back at the hotel we take a late supper and our *terrine de faisan* starter served with a sweet raisin *jus* and tiny pickled vegetables is delicious. My wife follows this with beefsteak grilled by *Monsieur* himself over another well-behaved open wood fire while my noisettes of duck with roasted apple and winter vegetables are exceptional. This is followed by the local *fromage* and afterwards, a pear charlotte, light as a feather with a shiny dark chocolate sauce to dip into. A recommended local Chinon is a little lighter than expected but still a fine accompaniment to a truly delicious meal.

…and so to bed.

Nord Pas de Calais

13th March   Lumbres near St Omer   Le Moulin de Mombreaux

After a more interesting drive up from the Loire blighted only by more ghastly wind turbines, we arrive in St Omer in the early afternoon ready for a dawn attack on the Calais Ferry port. Familiar battlefield names roll by and the countryside is altogether more interesting. We had considered a slightly shorter route via Paris but decided to keep that particular experience for later and anyway we'll probably go by TGV in preference to using the car.

Le Moulin de Mombreaux is exactly that - an old watermill with an impressive force, which was originally diverted by means of a lock gate to drive the mill wheel and in the restaurant the substantial wooden axels and gears, bearing the patina that only age and use can bestow, occupy pride of place. This is a much more modern affair than Chinon's Le Haut Clos and thoroughly deserves its additional star. Whilst the hotel is more up market it will really have to impress in order to improve on the marks awarded for last night's dinner.

With just one night's stop there is so much less to do so the afternoon is dedicated to light administration and observing the ducks. It's silly but I'm always happy when I see Mallards. Le Moulin's ducks populate the stream's banks where they promenade and noisily hold court before bobbing and dabbling in the water. In my male prejudice it always seems entirely appropriate that the lacklustre brown females take second place to the brightly coloured males, following them about two or three steps behind. Cautiously I decide not to mention this.

Later my wife spots an otter in the distance but it quickly rounds a bend in the stream and is lost to sight before I have a chance to see it.

We dine late on *haute cuisine*. The *menu du jour* comprised an interesting egg and fresh salmon confection served in shells; delicious but a work of questionable art and all held together on a bed of pink salt which, we are assured, is for decoration only. The *plat*, charred supreme of chicken accompanied by *ratatouille* wrapped in a crisp pancake, was delicious but begged the question just how the chef had managed to retain the pancake's crispness as it enveloped all those moist vegetables. Dessert was a selection of *crème brulee* of a delightful lightness. We drank stunningly good Bordeaux, a Mouton Cadet that just happened to be on offer and therefore could not be refused. Judgement was reserved on the better meal.

Later as we return to our room we meet a recently arrived English couple who have horror stories regarding storm and strike chaos at the Ferry terminal to impart and so decide to get away earlier in the morning.

14th March   Calais

I hold to my earlier stated view that Calais was greatly better ordered when under medieval English rule!

Arriving indecently early having met not one single obstruction, impediment or barrier to progress on the way we present ourselves at Emigration Control Calais, which alone in France is situated on the correct side of the vehicle. Here we are scrutinised by a professionally sceptical eye while at the same time our passports are scanned by an equally cynical infernal machine. Having passed muster but clearly only just, we present ourselves at the next hurdle. At the ferry booking-in point we manage to remember our Reference Number and also have Darcey's Pet Passport to hand since it is she who is partly to blame for our unseemly premature arrival. *Madame* discovers us within the depths of her computing device and while clearly disapproving the notion that there is An Animal Passenger in our car, brandishes a microchip reader in reluctant acknowledgement of the fact. My wife flusters to protect poor Darcey from this vile slur but like her Master, the dog is as deaf as a post and thus unconcerned, so she need not have bothered. Motivated both by national pride and the defence of dogdom, I trump *Madame's* ace with Darcey's Pet Passport. *Madame* curls a lip, considers her cards, sneers and takes the trick - pointing out that, as anyone with an iota of common sense should know, in order to travel legally to the UK, Darcey must have had Tick treatment and a Tapeworm injection both within the last 48 hours and as her passport clearly shows, this has not taken place. This being so the aforementioned Animal Passenger may not travel. QED!

Darcey? Ticks! Tapeworms! Heaven forfend! My wife places her hands over the dog's ears and turns her face to the wall in wretched mortification. Meanwhile I am adjudged by most of those assembled the sole representative of the He Has Not One Jot of Common Sense Circle (*Provisionals*) and therefore not to be trusted. Without a vote being taken my wife is immediately and unanimously appointed officer-in-charge of things to do with Darcey's Pet Passport and I find it prudent to remember that at all times.

While we fluster and panic starts to set in, *Madame* has communicated with a Higher Authority and frankly, for all that I loathe and detest bureaucracy in all its manifest forms, in this instance Higher Authority could not have been more helpful. Summoned to an inner sanctum I fully expect to be accorded a minimum of time and wisdom and a great deal of Gallic condescension and

106

clearly in the wrong, am hard pressed not to genuflect - but no! We are greeted politely and in a matter of mere moments The Rules are explained, a list of local veterinary surgeons together with a photostat street map of Calais produced, and our booking effortlessly transferred to 24 hours later. Commiserations and 'Thank goodness you've a GPS' sentiments are expressed, and manoeuvred with consummate skill from the premises, we are dispatched forthwith to the Veterinarian Surgeon.

At the Vet's surgery and still before 8:30 in the morning, *Monsieur* is incredibly businesslike, incredibly charming and incredibly young and resolves our predicament in an incredible five minutes flat from a standing start. It actually takes him more time to check and update the passport than administer the treatment and relieved of a sizeable quantity of hard cash, we return to Lumbres to beg another night's accommodation because Darcey is not allowed to travel until 24 hours have elapsed. During our return I start to wonder if things were not just a little pat and rehearsed and whether I deserve my appointment as founder member of the No Common Sense Circle (*P*) or if others have trod this particular Yellow Brick Road before me. I hold this notion in the breast for fear of further sneering. At least that's my excuse and I'm sticking to it through thick and thin. Apart from the normal outrage regarding her unwarranted treatment at the hands of the Vet, Darcey sleeps peacefully on, blissfully unaware of the consternation she has caused.

Meanwhile back at Lumbres a second night's accommodation is booked and we spend a rather pleasant day doing nothing more strenuous than lightly exploring Calais and enjoying another landmark dinner at Le Moulin de Mombreaux.

The jury is still out regarding the finer points of the respective cuisines of Le Moulin and Le Haut Clos. Le Moulin has it on style and technical content but Le Haut Clos is ahead on artistic merit. There will be further culinary consideration never fear!

15th March   Calais

At the second time of asking we negotiate the Ferry Port's bureaucracy with ease and to highlight the event I am allowed to play with the microchip reader - another first. Yet again we have arrived with far too much time in hand but it being a Saturday and business a little slack, a nice P&O gentleman assigns us to an earlier half empty sailing and consequently we arrive in the UK ahead of ourselves.

15th March   Dover

Once again the procedures at the Dover ferry Port are straightforward and undemanding until, that is, the Government interferes; as governments are prone to do.

We disembark in record time and then sit in an interminable queue to see if we've qualified for a surly HM Customs inspection. Arriving eventually in a gloomy, made to order hangar, which spans the road, the attendant Customs Officers are professionally qualified doubters. Aided and abetted by brusque police officers who lurk about in fluorescent coats with their hands in their pockets, they clearly resent the fact that they and we, are there at all. I just know that what they really want to do is to shoot someone with a Taser. My wife tells me to shut up before I am arrested.

We pass odd bays off where The Unfortunates are to be seen standing forlornly beside their vehicles while, employing the full majesty of the law, depressing Authority pries. In as much as one can be inconspicuous in a line of traffic we steal through but much like driving past a speed camera and even though we have not imported anything, feel guilty by association and are thankful not to be intercepted and subjected to impassive intimidation.

Thankfully we emerge and attempt to leave the docks but departure is further delayed when masses of lorries, coaches and cars are focussed into one single lane via an assembly of traffic cones and all roads eventually converge, not on Rome, but on a wholly inadequate roundabout. Much Flocking is evident but as this is England it is restrained and lacks the continental uproar. Throughout this hushed bedlam uniformed policemen, arms crossed, look on from the sideline - traffic jams clearly being nothing to do with them.

Surveillance, speed traps, traffic chaos, over mighty bureaucracy; we seriously wonder why we bothered to come home at all.

When we eventually reach it the motorway is packed with the lorries that we were told about in France. Mile after mile of HGVs line the opposite carriageways with more arriving by the minute.

The motorway home is quite busy for a Saturday and

congested around London because of extensive road works but we plod on manfully, eventually reaching home in the early afternoon. We knew we'd reached our particular stretch of motorway - it's cobbled!

Finale

So why did we bother? After all the entire trek was considerably more expensive than a fly/drive excursion and in some respects more arduous. In a nutshell, it all came down to our determination to enjoy a month away as a family simply enjoying longer winter days in better weather, a rather pleasant reconnaissance of our chosen Mediterranean *départements* and some fairly random house hunting. In our case *en famille* perforce included the dog. As for travelling light, just for a change we were able to take much more luggage and frankly at the end of the day found that we didn't need the half of it.

Ferries

Irrespective of my apparent disapprobation the outbound Sea France ferry crossing was actually first-class and cheap at twice the price. Due to the atrocious weather, courtesy of the tail end of a tropical storm which audaciously ventured across the Atlantic, we returned to the UK a couple of days early and aboard a P&O Ferry because Sea France had decided to have a strike that prevented us booking with them once more. My wife wondered if they knew I was coming. In the event, it was a fortunate turn of events. I often contemplate if another company's foreign representatives would have shown such excellent customer service when faced with weary travellers on the cusp of mutiny and their irregular uninjected undocumented Animal Passenger.

The P&O supervisor who sorted out Darcey's pet passport problem at Calais was a Godsend and a fine ambassador for his company and later I wrote to tell them so. The young French Vet was hugely amused and absolutely charming - something I simply could not have achieved before breakfast and in a foreign language.

Driving

Initially the long distance driving was tiring but only I think, because I was out of practice and it has to be said that the new car took much of the strain. I'm grateful to Saab for constructing such reliable and comfortable cars. Ours performed superbly and top up or down, gave not one moment's concern.

Whilst I paid it only passing tribute the GPS machine, for all its little idiosyncrasies, was an absolute Godsend and in the presence of this congregation, I now confess that my occasional complaints were sometimes specious. A friend had bought one to assist his periodic driving work and when he showed it off it in our kitchen one afternoon I was sceptical and accused him of laziness. The TomTom GPS we bought was a hugely useful driving accessory particularly in built up areas and made navigation so much easier but, and there is always a 'but', it is prone to exploring inappropriate byways in search of the shortest route and has to be carefully monitored to avoid *interesting* detours.

Rereading what I'd written about British motorways I would not withdraw one word. They are an absolute disgrace and it's a sad reflection on government that all out national infrastructure compares so badly with the continent and on us all for putting up with it. I really could not understand why our motorways are being measured in kilometres and if they must be, why such expensive signs and posts have been used when a much more subtle and I imagine cheaper, variation is used abroad.

The cost benefit of using the French toll motorways is difficult to quantify. In some respects by avoiding them we would certainly have seen a lot more of rural France. On the other hand we'd been fairly careful in planning the various stages and their convenience was obvious. When we visit again we've decided to spend a little less time travelling on them and in the light of experience, have promised to build a little more flexibility into the programme. There was so much we just did not see - but that's being wise after the event.

Supermarkets

Other conveniences of our stay were the various supermarkets, which were more often than not, fairly ready to hand. Now, I admit I am no expert but based on empirical evidence, I found the various Leclerc and Carrefour establishments a tad more agreeable and certainly more interesting than their British counterparts. I have to confess that to my mind one supermarket is much like another. Like some great apparatus, deliveries of food and goods enters the building by one door, are sorted, displayed, selected and purchased within and exit through another, and the only variable is the way that the store and chain is marketed. I have absolutely no doubt that my wife who is officer-in-charge of these matters has a different view since she tends to be the one who does the shopping and therefore spends more time in them. I have noticed that she has preferences both by handiness and product, preferring one for meat another for booze and a third for a quick drop-in shop. The consequence is that for most of the time she knows what it is that she wants, where it is to be found and roughly how much it will cost.

The stores we patronised in France were a new experience and we needed to digest the what, where and how much factors on the hoof - or at least on the trolley - or risk spending hours wandering about in a hopeless muddle. Fortunately we were able to develop a fairly clear method to temper the complications. All our lettings started on a Saturday so we attempted to leave the previous cottage about 10 am, drive the four or so hours to the next, where, arriving about 2 pm we would unpack the car, quickly find a convenient supermarket and replenish those items of immediate need or that could not travel. To make life a little easier we tended to eat out over the weekends, which in the culinary centre of the world, was a real hardship.

The 'Where' and 'How much' issues were but a minor nuisance; the 'What' had the potential for real fun and games. We tended to stick to convenience food; tins of this, jars of that and bearing in mind the status of our French, thank goodness for the stores' marketing folk who, largely ignoring the current fashion for perplexing healthy labels, stuck coloured photographs of the various containers' contents on them. For obvious reasons this methodology tended to falter at the delicatessen counter but being an irredeemable nibbler, I was able to purchase any number of fresh commodities based entirely on grazing experience and we enjoyed them all. The wide varieties of local vegetables and salads were stunningly good and we particularly liked the availability of choice and that handfuls of this and sprigs of that were to be had. The fish counters were spectacular and the many varieties, some new to us, quite amazing. The wine departments were a joy and a lot of my time was spent among their convivial stacks inspecting the runners and riders snuggled companionably on their shelves. Mostly the wines were arranged by region, domain and price but there was always a comprehensive local selection and so we were able to try some excellent *vins de pays* quickly and without too much advanced local knowledge.

I liked the idea of other outlets and franchises being available within the premises; some more than others but all more or less pitched against a perceived need or marketing trend. Often there was an excellent baker so we were able to try any number of different breads and cartwheels of pastries without struggling into the town and fighting to park.

When we take up residence we'll probably use local shops and markets but, while the arguments for and against out of town stores rages on, we're very grateful that, for the moment, they're there and available.

Location – location!

It's difficult to conclude that any one destination was better than another as all were individual with their own virtues and vices and in the end it was weather rather than location that defeated us. We enjoyed Provence north and south and Aquitaine was charming but have decided that, rugged and windy though it can be, we'll probably settle in the Aude when we finally sell up and move to France to live. The lure of the Mediterranean is difficult to refute.

Civics

It might be construed that I'm unsympathetic to green issues as I was critical of wind turbines and speed bumps and this deserves further explanation. It's not the concept but the application that bothers me. It seems to me that the French are planting wind turbines by the acre with precious little thought to the environment or their efficiency and I fear that we will shortly follow suit. Quite why these monstrous eyesores could not be consigned to rafts at sea is beyond me.

Similarly I have no problem with appropriate traffic calming measures and speed bumps but I do have a problem with the excesses of height and occasional absence of proper warning of the French versions and fear that many of them, both in France and the UK, are manufactured for fashion rather than as an essential requirement.

Wherever we went I was much impressed with the attitude to rubbish disposal both by the creators and the collectors, and it always seemed to work well.

Flocking

Just in case I am to be accused of frivolity, the Flocking Behaviour theory is absolutely genuine and from my unscientific experience, holds up to critical evaluation. I would draw readers' attention to the work of Craig

116

Reynolds and others regarding the characteristics of: Separation, Alignment and Cohesion. An interesting Flocking Simulator can be found on the Internet for those who really must.

Whilst on the subject, the young German *Bundeswehr* officer I described was so embarrassed that having knocked a chunk off his immaculate tank, the disaster was compounded by it having failed to dent the concrete block. It was a real struggle to keep a straight face and I'm certain that his crew of conscripts felt much the same.

Tourism

All the B&Bs and Logis de France hotels were standardly good and I was hugely struck by the care an attention lavished on us by their respective staff. Their concept of quality service is authentic and not some capricious marketing exercise, as is so often the case in the UK. Folk were standardly polite, tidy and professional and clearly cared about what they were doing. And the food…!

Having run out of time we failed to return to Avignon but are using that as a rather thin excuse to go back in future. The car parking there really was as bad as I described and is something they ought to address.

The Guide Michelin was, as ever, hugely useful but we did notice a distinct difference between the format of the Provence and Languedoc - Roussillon versions. The former seemed much more user friendly but while the latter contained just as much information it was that much harder to access. You'd have thought the guides would have a standard configuration but no - and that lack of consistency ought to be considered by the publishers.

We loved both the French habit of naming their motorways and the EU inspired brown tourist signposts to be found on them. Some iconic, others pictorial they seemed more inspired than the British variety celebrating as they do, each town and city's essential character.

Now is the time for another confession; the Ardèche Gorge scared me rigid. When we return I shall stick to the canoeing and avoid the heights.

We adored the various seaside locations and Sanary sur Mere was a joy. Our Government really should do something practical about the parlous state of the British fishing industry.

...and the cottages? Without exception the owners were enthusiastic and keen to show off their particular and much loved parts of France. They were all well equipped and cared for and competitively priced. We of course were well out of season and I did observe that availability and price changed as summer and the school holidays advanced. Well they would wouldn't they?

Everyone at home who knew we were 'doing' France seemed fascinated beforehand and were similarly interested to know how we'd got on when we returned. We've almost developed a script to cope with their curiosity.

Postscript

The dog Darcey Bussell, for all her little inconveniences, had a great time abroad and so did we, which was just as well. Not long after arriving home we discovered a lump in her throat and jaw, which, despite first class treatment, had within a fortnight, spread to alarming proportions. The decision to put her to sleep was not difficult.

'And, my friend, when I am very old, and I no longer enjoy good health, hearing and sight, do not make heroic efforts to keep me going. I am no longer having any fun. Please see that my trusting life is taken gently. I shall leave this earth knowing with the last breath I draw that my fate was always safest in your hands.'

Treat Me Kindly.
Beth Norman Harris 1968.

I have reproduced her poem in full as an appendix.

Book Two

No Criticisms

'Animals are such agreeable friends – they ask no questions, they pass no criticisms.'

George Eliot

A rose between two thorns

Painting by Penny Richardson

Exordium

Post hoc, ergo propter hoc

After this, therefore because of this

A sophism

Whilst it has absolutely nothing to do with light-hearted trips abroad or dogs, or frankly much else beyond mystifying studies in philosophy, I've always been rather fond of the *Post hoc* proposition. At first flush this might seem an odd and perhaps rather obscure idea with which to commence this book but please bear with me, given all the evidence that follows I claim just cause and sufficient grounds.

For the benefit of untutored undergraduates (*...and The Great Unwashed, among whose proud ranks I am regularly to be found numbered*) *Post hoc's* premise is usually described as meaning that one event having preceded another, it therefore follows that the first incident was the cause of the second. In intellectual circles the concept is denounced – more often in magisterial tones, superior style and academic gown - as a plausible but essentially mistaken argument.

Not entirely unexpectedly, in the Real World Beyond The Lecture Hall, *Post hoc's* dented hypothesis is occasionally and conveniently, reversed. Thus, should a future outcome be considered disagreeable then taking steps to avoid the first event will prevent it - as if?

So, in the absence of anything better, here's a *hoc* or two worthy of further *dégustation...*

Chapter One

......*and it came to pass*

Whoever said you can't buy happiness forgot little puppies

Gene Hill.

Elle has entered our lives with the force and disruptive power of a miniature hurricane.

Losing a faithful companion such as Darcey had been simply dreadful but, as you do, we put on a brave show and having achieved a certain time of life, were determined to create opportunity from misfortune - resolving to Do Things Differently In Future.

On the plus side, without a dog in the house the kitchen and hall were noticeably cleaner, there was a marked absence of dog hair and canine artefacts about the place and, as our friends pointed out, the potential for spur-of-the-moment trips abroad beckoned. On the other hand a certain glumness prevailed so, in order to cheer us up and take our minds off dear old Darcey, a cheap last minute fly-drive to Eymet just south of Bergerac was organised. Our friends reasoned that a few days touring the Dordogne while based in a medieval township would be just the thing ...and it was!

The short stay in an English owned B&B in the company of our friends was more than agreeable, Eymet, a small slice of medieval England *en* France, delightful and the surrounding area simply charming. Had we but realised the region's potential, our earlier curtailed wet week in the vineyards of Saint Émilion north of La

Dordogne might have been rescued by a detour a little further south of Bergerac and the river. The once ecclesiastical stronghold of Issigeac with its bishop's palace; Beaumont and Monpazier, antique fortified hilltop *Bastides*, the New Towns of the Middle Ages, these all deserved much more than the fleeting inspection we gave them but, we agreed, therein lies opportunity.

Thus time progressed, still dogless and truth be told, badly missing the companionship, we continued to rationalise the huge gap in our lives little realising that around us our small community were making a book on when we'd founder.

The dog walking gang continued its daily trek *sans* Darcey and much to the amusement of walkers, owners and many other interested parties, I found myself greeting and admiring any and every available dog on our way.

A long weekend in mainland Spain to visit friends made an enjoyable interlude and a fortnight's break in Mallorca, arranged for late September and early October, was a pleasant prospect serving to lift our spirits. Arriving home without a frantic tail wagging greeting just inside the front door regularly lowered them again.

That summer on the pretence of essential but woefully overdue maintenance, I found myself engaged in auditing various files on the computer's Internet Browser, a housekeeping chore I heartily loathe. Therein awaiting rediscovery lurked a folder entitled 'Dogs' and within, loitering with intent, the Web address of the Jack Russell Club of Great Britain. Affecting disinterest and based on the very thin excuse that no harm could possibly be done in just checking that it was still live, I made the

123

connection…

Until health, finance and political correctness forced me to give up the pleasure I enjoyed smoking cigars. One late autumn evening in a Perpignan cafe, having long since abstained, we were enjoying an *après* dinner drink and observing other customers smoking and clearly enjoying it, I weakened. 'No harm in just one' thought I. No doubt you can guess the rest.

…one of the pages that appeared on the screen before me was a list of breeders and next thing, just for interest you understand, I caught myself scouring every one of them for puppies, re-homing opportunities and rescues. With Satan hovering at my shoulder and sorely tempted my sins of commission grew progressively worse - but at least I wasn't smoking.

Meanwhile Eve was likewise beguiled since, unbeknown to me, my wife was engaged in similar moral weaknesses. Dear Reader, the Serpent was abroad in Orchard House and neither of us knew it. In the way of all things imperfect the truth eventually emerged and, confession being good for the soul, we agreed to combine our efforts. We are, it has to be admitted, inveterate doggy folk.

Chapter Two

'Happiness Is A Warm Puppy.'

Charles M Schultz.

August

Darcey had died shortly after our return home from France and by employing every weak pretext known we manfully resisted replacing her but had weakened by the late summer of that year.   In August I had made contact with a breeder of Parson Russell Terriers in the Midlands and; 'Yes there had been a litter' and: 'Yes there was one female still available' and: 'Yes we could come and see her' and: 'Yes tomorrow would be fine!'

In the interim it seemed to us that Tomorrow Never Comes but in the fullness of time *Post hoc*, naturally it did. In due course, much like kids let loose in a sweetshop, we found ourselves in deepest Leicestershire closely examining and in my case energetically cuddling, eight week old Homstar Fennella progeny of Jagen Johnny Riplington and Ardencote Tiva of Alne.   She is such a pretty little waif and we are captivated. Our friends said later that had the poor animal been born with horns and a cloven hoof we'd have had her, and of course they were right.   What cold-hearted swine could resist puppy breath and a small white cuddle that squirmed in delight at the attention while simultaneously inserting a coarse wet tongue gently into your ear?   The dog is all white, broken coated with one brown piratical eyebrow and, as the breeder proudly explains, well conformed with a good temperament, a proud lineage and in comparison with the rest of the litter, the heart of a lion. The puppy's sire is a champion but her dam Tiva, has only been sparingly shown and thus lacks form; nevertheless she is an attractive and attentive mother. This bodes well and although my wife is nominally officer-in-charge, I have read the runes and prepare to part with more money.

A word or two about Jack Russell's terriers might be useful. The Reverend John Russell (*1795-1883*), scion of a West Country fox hunting family and later the popular vicar of the Devonshire village of Swimbridge, was a hunting man in his own right as well as a founder of the Kennel Club but for all that he is more often remembered as the breeder of the popular little terriers that bear his name to this day.

The story goes that whilst up at Oxford and already prone to spending excessive time out riding to hounds, the young undergraduate spotted and bought a local milkman's pet dog; a cross breed that closely suited his requirement for a working terrier that could run all day with foxhounds yet was small and brave enough to flush out earthed foxes. Having found his ideal prototype he successfully bred and worked these dogs for the remainder of his long life.

After his death enthusiasts continued to develop the breed and inevitably its characteristics gradually changed, so that nowadays there are two distinct varieties of John Russell's dogs to be found. Fans of both bloodlines tend to be ardent devotees, even to the extent of international skirmishing over their names - on which subject there is a rather juicy tale of intrigue, closely guarded title ownership and Kennel Club recognition to be told, but not here!

And so:

'In the red corner - Parson Russell Terriers.' These dogs are deliberately bred so as to reflect and preserve the original, compact, rather leggy working dog that John Russell would recognise today.

'...and in the blue - Jack Russell Terriers.' Rather better known, these dogs are the Parsons' shorter, Queen Anne legged and equally determined, hybrid cousins.

Within the somewhat snobbish world of pedigree dogs and only after a close contest eventually won on points, it is the Parson Russell Terrier that is recognised by the UK Kennel Club nowadays.

Breeding notwithstanding each in their turn are neat intelligent dogs that can be and often are, inclined to stubbornness. Given to dense weatherproof coats that can vary between smooth and rough, all Russells are bred to be predominantly white but frequently have shades of bronze and black markings, preferably on the head and about the base of the tail. Traditionally docked - like fox hunting, a practice now discontinued - these days they retain their rather ratty unrestrained tails. Good around horses, so often described as stable dogs, these are friendly, devoted and affectionate little animals with bags of personality. They do well with children and make smashing pets for active folk. Whilst avoiding most of the breeding shortcomings that plague and disfigure some pedigree dogs, they are agile, lively and make great ratters. Russells, all of them, love to dig, climb and chew so, and as will be seen, potential owners who are house proud and keen gardeners should take careful heed.

There is an expression to be found in the Kennel Club's Parson Russell Terrier breed standard, which complements Jerome's 'original sin' description and goes far to typify these plucky little characters. It reads: 'Honourable scars permitted.'

🐕 🐕

It transpired that the puppy would be ready to be collected just a couple of weeks before we were due to depart for a Mediterranean holiday and unhappy to take her just to leave her kennelled or with friends at a critical time in her development, we were grateful that the breeder was prepared to hold young Fennella until we returned from our fortnight in the sun. So money changed hands and we arranged to collect her on the day after we were due back.

A week later my wife rang the breeder to check on the

dog's progress and to announce that after much deliberation young Fennella, currently responding quite happily to 'Puppy' and 'Hey You', was hereinafter to be known as Elle.

Accordingly the 12th October was known as E Day and the countdown had begun.

Early October 2008.

We arrived home from our delightful Mallorcan holiday very late and very tired on a cold wet Saturday night to an utterly dismal Liverpool airport where, as usual, the Lords of Disruption and Mismanagement reigned. Frankly the combination of invasive security, ghastly officialdom and penny-pinching airline organization, both coming and going, has only strengthened my resolve never to travel by air again. Regrettably I am becoming a bore about such matters, completely overlooking the fact that the recipients of my invective have suffered much the same inconveniences. I am calmed and rescued from complete paroxysm by my wife's reminder that tomorrow is E Day.

It's been years since we've coped with a puppy and a two weeks fitness regime at delightful Porto Petro has, I sincerely hope, prepared me for the fray. Twice daily sea bathing is remarkably strengthening, although I discovered that swimming through a shoal of jellyfish - something akin to going for a dip in stinging nettles - diminished my enjoyment more than a little. The staff of a local diving school, German to a man and professionally acquainted with the problem but miffed that I'd even dared to ask if they spoke English, quickly took pity and relented. Thus this mottled victim, now reassured of no danger to life and gratefully in possession of the remedy, spent the remainder of the day dowsed in malt vinegar and smelling much like ambulatory cod and chips.

We worked hard, ate well, slept for England and made new friends. Cheap at twice the price.

At Orchard House unpacked and unwound we managed bed by threeish but were both up and doing before eight at which time it took great effort to prevent my wife, who it will be remembered is officer-in-charge of such matters, telephoning the breeders there and then to let them know we were coming. In the event and only after much convincing, a call at a more civilised hour was made when it transpired that a dog show was ordained to interfere with our plans and Elle could be collected about teatime. 'Would this be OK?'

'Of course it will.' said my wife sweetly through a fixed smile and grinding teeth.

The Sunday afternoon drive down to rural Leicestershire in the Saab was enjoyably traffic free; with a late pub lunch taken *en route* to waste a little time before our appointed arrival time. At the breeder's the lady of the house made us welcome but we sensed a certain gloom among those assembled at the prospect of Elle's imminent departure. The dog having grown somewhat, was as biddable and delightful as before so I could understand why and commiserate, but not overly much.

We'd loaded Darcey's house in anticipation but in the event, young Madam settled herself on my wife's lap and slept for the duration of the return journey occasionally cocking a bleary eye when traffic halted. This was an exciting prospect, a docile tractable puppy; perhaps our common futures would be a little less demanding than we'd anticipated.

On arriving home and even though it's Sunday afternoon, the local Pet Supermarket is open for business so equipping for the new puppy is not difficult. In not much time at all my credit card is significantly dented and together with the puppy we are the proud owners of: a collar; engraved identity disks; a lead; various bowls; food; a sleeping box; an essential breed book which Just Had To Be Bought; and …and the list goes on. Elle who is now awake and paying attention, kindly agrees to be carried round the store in a rucksack that hitherto lived in the Saab's boot and contained all the now redundant, creature comforts and necessities required for opportunistic nights away. Her head and front paws emerge, rather like an upright and very inquisitive tortoise, consequently she is admired outrageously and, a warning for the future, loves every minute of it.

…and so to Orchard House.

All our reading on puppy management strongly recommends a Start As You Mean To Go On regime and so we are determined to follow that advice. In the interim administration takes over. Elle's ownership is painlessly transferred on the Kennel Club's web site albeit at a price which at least comes with the benefit of six week's complimentary pet insurance that buys some breathing space before we have to worry about it again. An appointment with the vet is arranged for registration and an initial MoT examination to take place on the morrow. Thereafter Madam is fed, watered and introduced to the garden's toilet facilities. Thankfully she's had the benefit of a longer than usual stay with the breeder and their dogs, so toilet training is almost there already.

After a long couple of days we are all more than ready for an early night so, starting as we mean to go on, we weaken immediately and Elle - who until now has been used to sleeping alongside the warm bulk of a large hound and is bound to feel lonely - shares the bed where she immediately snuggles down and blissfully sleeps the night through.

It's been some months since our last visit but next morning at our local vet's we are greeted like long lost and much missed friends. This warmth is, I suspect, more to do with the prospect of regular injections of additional working capital than any eager anticipation of my brilliant wit and sparkling repartee. Elle is once more *en* rucksack and the young lady partner who sees us departs gleefully to the inner sanctums with Elle in her backpack and shortly delight is audibly evident among the assembled but invisible female staff off stage. On her return our new Superstar is suitably modest and the carrier has been rechristened the Doggy Bag. Thereafter following much hateful examination, endured without too much protest, the puppy is pronounced sound in wind and limb; after which I pay up manfully, wince, and we depart.

I appreciate that long explanations of the blood sweat and tears, worries, and sheer fun relating to the introduction of a puppy into a household might just be old hat to many who have managed to stay with the plot thus far - so I shall resist the temptation.

Except to say that we more or less got things right; much as I suspect old puppy hands might agree. No doubt purists could take issue with our methodology - there are many valid opinions on the subject. They may also have reservations about our abandoning professional training classes after three visits in favour of doing it ourselves, but in and among the occasional accidents, chewing of the kitchen stools, a comprehensive review of sleeping arrangements in a downstairs training cage, an infestation of worms and other, rather less offensive, canine topics things progressed tolerably well.

In short order and with much juvenile ingratiation, Elle had become firmly established as part of the family.

Chapter Three

'Parsons are like chocolates - you can't stop at one.'

Linda Bigland. Heythrop Terriers

When you've been married for over forty years you get to know when Something's On Her Mind. She Who Must Be Obeyed, quite casually mind you, has suggested that a brace of Parson Russell Terriers might be a good idea. This is a new departure and if I'm honest the same thing has crossed my mind, however in the face of wistful feminine desire, I'm keeping *stumm*. Enquiries are to be made - just to test the water you understand.

In keeping with the *Post hoc* hypothesis it turns out that, by sheer coincidence, a well-known breeder of Elle's bloodline has a six-month old dog available for rehoming. Enquiries reveal that the lad was retained to show but one of his testicles has failed to descend and this defect has effectively put paid to that cunning plan. Since we've no intentions of showing or breeding, his minor shortcoming presents no problems for us; perhaps we could call him Hitler? In the event we waver and since 'He who hesitates is lost', miss the opportunity, so young Adolph goes merrily off to a good home elsewhere. We wonder what his new family will call him?

This is a setback but sophism or not, *Post hoc* is not to be denied and almost immediately another six-month old Parson is advertised. In much the same circumstances as Hitler albeit at the other end of his architecture, this lad's bite is slightly crooked putting paid to his chances in the

134

show ring.

We are now convinced …we have almost persuaded ourselves …somebody thought it might be a good idea.

Once bitten we are determined not to dither again so by appointment and in not too much time at all, take ourselves off to hunting country on the edge of the Cotswolds and that very same day, *ergo propter hoc*, Heythrop Trust Monty with his crooked bite and appealing manner, is bought and sold.

Elle has made the trip down consigned to Darcey's house on the back seat of the Saab. Since the essential canine introductions, vital before they set off for home together, result in a minor Mexican stand-off but with more teeth, there she stays, whilst the lad gets snuggling rights in the front with my wife. Clearly having won the first round on points he settles down and sleeps for the entire journey. Elle is not amused.

'Trusty?' 'Monty?' 'Hey You?' The lad is a good-looking typical Parson but unlike Elle he has much more colour about his head and tail with some shadowy ticking evident under his smooth white coat. The dog has an attractive coppery, light brunette and white face, dark soulful eyes, and a rather raffish air. He's clearly a Sam.

So Dear Reader there you have it; our very own, self-imposed poisoned chalice: '*Sam 'n' Ella*' - say it quickly.

…and then we were four

Apart from some blood and fur on Day One the pups have settled down *en famille* and have become firm, if competitive, friends. I confess we were more than a little concerned, even alarmed, at the spat but with the benefit of twenty-twenty hindsight, now recognise this juvenile brawl for what it was, merely an exercise in jockeying for status and position. Thankfully they've quickly settled down to life together and have become steadfast pals, even to the extent of moping when separated, which can be amusing.

Scene one: Elle to vets. Sam is discovered in an out-of-the-way kitchen corner having turned his face to the wall. He'd have a trembling bottom lip if his canine anatomy permitted it!

Scene two: Sam to vets. Elle retreats to bed in the now redundant training cage and, even with the lure of her favourite treats, will neither emerge nor acknowledge us, preferring to remain in a tight dismal curl of misery until the Lad returns.

🐕 🐕

There is sadness abroad in Orchard House. The Saab must go. Our first convertible, it's been a smashing car and has served us well but the pups' need more space than it provides, especially as we intend to take trips abroad with them. Being a two-door model it was always something of a trial getting Darcey in and out of her house unless the Saab's roof was down and, the whole being more than the sum of its parts, it poses a real problem with the two dogs.

Research for a suitable replacement commences. Given my low opinion of Dinkers and Dingers a more robust vehicle is preferred with Range Rovers or similar sport utility types heading the list. Since we both loved driving in the continental sunshine with the car's top

136

down, some sort of convertible would be a bonus. Weeks later we have crawled over an interminable host of SUV and various crossover vehicles but are no nearer to a resolution until that is the BBC's Top Gear Website comes to our rescue. Its suggestion that a hard top Jeep Wrangler model might meet our needs is deemed worthy of further investigation. This particular vehicle is not one we'd considered but we are attracted by the fact that it's sturdy, damn near undinkable, roomy and whilst not a soft-top convertible or a twin top, we can remove the front roof panels.

At the dealers I can't immediately see the Jeep of choice so I express my desire to view one. I am astonished to be greeted by much sucking of teeth and shaking of heads: 'Oh no Mr Long, none available; they're not to be had for love or money in the UK. We only get a few every year.' I am astounded and say so, but in the midst of my outrage: 'Hell's teeth - you're a Jeep dealer!' am adroitly manoeuvred in the direction of the much larger five door Jeep Wrangler. Frankly this fits all our requirements but is massive; so much so that I feel the need for a stable yard's mounting block just to climb aboard. Once Our Hero is installed behind the wheel it's rather like sitting in a tunnel but at least the roof comes off! Sensing my uncertainty the salesman plays a trump card; the price of this brand new Wrangler, he announces, has been discounted by fifty percent …then the Parthian Shot, this unmissable deal ends in a week's time. Chrysler man deftly takes the trick by offering a spectacularly good part exchange price for the Saab.

Overawed by such nimble sales technique we buy the beast and in short order are fully committed converts to the quirky Jeep brand.

Much later we had the opportunity to inspect a friend's smaller Wrangler and rather late in the day realize we've made the best choice by far. This Jeep's cargo space is much tighter, almost verging on the non-existent and we'd have reverted to the problem of two doors, two dogs and not much space for luggage. Our Manchester dealer is therefore accorded Gold Standard but, even when so commended, fails to discount the servicing charges and so is promptly demoted to Silver Gilt.

We've always been keen gardeners and have nurtured our Orchard House plot since we bought the property and its steep rubble-strewn grounds, brand new from the builders about seventeen years ago.

Elle & Sam in the garden

Painting by Penny Hanby

With its now well-established trees, shrubs, lawns, water features and a paved patio the size of a smaller regimental drill square, whilst no Villandry, it has been the scene of many memorable and fun filled, if rather boozy, garden parties. The lawns however have always needed special attention as our Pennine location can be rather sodden. This has always been a problem but with care, certainly not an insurmountable one.

That was before. The Guys have eaten one dwarf apple tree; the lawns now resemble a muddy, divot infested, amateur rugby pitch after a particularly hard season; and the once pristine patio is buried under muddy paw prints and a carnage of chewed sticks, bones and carefully selected toys. Our meticulously manicured hedging appears to have been bombarded. Nowadays the orchard wants only a whiff of cordite and the rattle of distant musketry to resemble The Somme 1916. Bless them!

The training cage has outlived its original purpose so we've installed a wooden toddler gate in the doorway between the hall and kitchen. This contraption ought to keep the Guys where they should be at night and when we're out. They've eaten its bars. At no little expense we install plastic pipe covers to disguise the damage. They eat them too. The latest modification is an all-metal version. My wife is presently at the hardware merchant purchasing more pipe covers.

We're home from a quick shopping expedition; while I park the Jeep on the drive my wife unlocks the front door and enters the house with her bags. Shortly I arrive indoors to find my wife in tears before the kitchen gate, the dogs within, heads to one side and ears cocked, gazing innocently at her while sitting paw deep in shredded newspaper. They've had huge fun scaling the breakfast table to discover the recycling cache. It takes much heroic effort comforting She Who Must Be Obeyed and volunteering to clean up the mess, while narrowly avoiding the pups being despatched to the dogs' home forthwith.

Chapter Four

'Properly trained, a man can be dog's best friend.'

Corey Ford

We would prefer that our dogs should not be shackled in leads and harness forever and allowed a little freedom to roam but there's a percentage problem. The Guys are all terrier and for eighty-five percent of the time will respond willingly and immediately to the recall whistle to gather at our feet before sitting for a treat. However, for the remaining fifteen percent there are vital hunting affairs that simply cannot wait and any notion of discipline goes completely out of their heads. There have been a couple of close calls. Frankly the thought of scouring Rivington Pike and the Pennine moors in the dark and wet searching in vain for them whilst they enjoy fun and games seeking out wild rabbits and small vermin just does not appeal.

Some commentators suggest that many Russells simply cannot ever be trusted off their leads. Even so, we are resolute in our intentions but since there are many stables and extensive sheep farming nearby, we remain cautious.

My wife is appointed officer-in-charge of essential: Sit; Stay; Down; and Heel commands and we *all* find it prudent to remember that. I undertake Recall and countryside obedience. Unlike the long-standing military principle of 'First knock them down and then build them up' - a concept about which I've always entertained a healthy scepticism - we are convinced that encouragement and persuasion is the best way by far to achieve the desired measure of obedience whilst retaining their attractive and natural Russell qualities and characteristics. Recalling little Darcey's woefully intimidated demeanour during her early days with us, our master plan is plenty of carrot and a total absence of stick.

In the event the Guys are moderately responsive to authority but occasionally there are times when we are close to despair. Fortunately we've access to a large fenced pasture on the moors above Orchard House and separately and together spend much time reinforcing good behaviour. As time progresses we have some success. At first Sam was overly interested in the local sheep, a worrying fascination, but we're delighted that he's now well in hand. Typical stable dogs they both sit readily, remain calm and are usually much admired, as the regular riding schools trot by. There are many novice riders hereabouts and this is important.

We have trusted them off their leads in the enclosed lea and nearby sunken lanes and often they are excellent but it's an edgy business. We spend much time and effort coaching them in Recall; but...!

Bamburgh revisited

Our friends have been making plans for trips away. The man of the house recently underwent a long overdue hip replacement and is clearly much the better for it; so the usually much maligned NHS has got something right for once. Because he can't fly for a while they've been thinking about an interim road trip around Scotland before returning to the Mediterranean's sun, sea and sangria.   Concurrently other neighbours have been skiing, sunning in the Canaries and are currently in Canada.   As expected the dogs have rather limited our opportunities to join in the fun but during one training session in the sunken lane, I began to wonder if a return to Point Cottages in Northumberland - whilst not quite having the Med's allure - might not be a pleasant interlude. I have another motive. The beach adjacent to Bamburgh's charming links golf club stretches for mile after empty mile of golden sand, with nearly unscalable cliffs, dunes and the sea creating exactly the sort of training ground the Guys need just now. There they can run free of their leads without much danger of interference by other dogs, getting lost or mauling our local hill sheep.

My wife is officer-in-charge of things to do with arranging trips to Point Cottages and I find it prudent to remember that at all times ...so terms and conditions agreed and a booking secured, on the appointed day the Jeep is packed for a long weekend away. Darcey's house and the training cage are dragooned back into service, and we make for the north-east.   The dogs are not consulted.

Point Cottages Bamburgh

The Bamburgh Castle Golf Club, 'Established 1904' as its only slightly exclusive clubhouse proudly proclaims, lies at the end of a meandering coastal lane a little above the village and has carefully preserved car parking for several prominent officers and its members. The Remainder are consigned to hard-core standings dotted at irregular intervals along the way. The Wyndings which, were it not for the intervening Budle Bay, would wander its lonely way to Holy Island some miles beyond, is a well kept secret, maintained and preserved by a freemasonry of bird watchers, dog walkers and golfers.

The beach is an ever changing adventure, having rugged low lying coal seamed rocky outcrops to be explored when the tide is up and the North Sea crashes its force ashore, and miles of unbroken, sea bird patrolled, golden sand at low water. The Farne Islands lie directly offshore to the south east and, a source of much local pride, there is an interesting triangle of medieval castles, with the much restored Lindisfarne and Bamburgh nearby and Dunstanburgh, still in ruins, well to the south.

During the early 20th century Sir Edwin Lutyens remodelled Lindisfarne castle in Arts and Craft style while his partner in crime, Gertrude Jekyll, replanted the garden. It is entirely possible that this makeover was the most significant episode in Lindisfarne's rather unrewarding history.

In the meantime William Armstrong - engineer, arms manufacturer and local boy made good - knocked Bamburgh's castle about a bit, transforming it into a desirable Edwardian gentleman's residence of imposing character. Compared with poor uninspired Lindisfarne, Bamburgh's claim to fame was an early 15th century Wars of the Roses siege. In early summer 1464 after much effort in the ranks, Richard Neville the 'Kingmaker' Earl of Warwick reduced the beleaguered Lancastrian garrison's commander Sir Ralph Grey to eating his horse, before knocking him senseless with a cannonball - and then reducing his castle.

We've been returning here off and on for ten years and with the spirit of earlier endeavours firmly in mind, consider it will make an ideal venue for dog training.

In the event the Guys love every minute and so do we. Elle, it transpires, is a natural water baby but Sam, although blessed with many other fine doggy attributes, turns out to be an aquatic wimp.

We are able to allow them to run free and achieve much training success; though there was a heart-stopping moment when Sam scrambled up an almost sheer cliff in order to enjoy a moment or two on the golf club's ninth tee with the players and rabbits before ever considering the difficulty of his descent.

Bamburgh Beach

Chapter Five

Encore!

We're on a countdown at Orchard House. My wife has been considering a National Service style chuff chart to hang in the kitchen. France again! ...but only a holiday this time. After serious and prolonged deliberation and much agonised debate we have decided not to forsake Orchard House and merry England for France's Mediterranean coast. The reasons are many and varied, and for anyone savouring our doggy tales, probably as fascinating and enjoyable as a protracted head cold, so I shall not dwell on them further.

🐕 🐕

Amid the bleak mid-winter our traditional and eagerly anticipated Christmas repast - with all the usual trimmings and the now long-established decanter of Chinon - was thoroughly and unashamedly, enjoyed. This is the Guys' second Yuletide at home so, when not actively engaged in close supervision in the kitchen, they pursued convention, toasting themselves before the drawing room fire whilst we dined by candlelight and a thick layer of unexpected uncustomary and I imagine, globally warmed, snow camouflaged the wreck of the garden.

During a well-earned pause in the preparations we had discovered an excellent alternative to our usual French holiday cottage Internet portal and forthwith, booked accommodation at Istres, just West of Marseilles, for the whole of the month of March. We shall then drive over to Aquitaine to fulfil our promise of further exploration of the region's *Bastides* and have arranged a cottage at Plaisance, just South of Bergerac between Eymet and Issigeac, for a fortnight.

The tortuous and lengthy processes necessary to secure the Guys' pet passports have been completed and ours, only discovered at the very last minute to be on the cusp of expiry, have been renewed.

Much plotting and planning has taken place. My wife has been brushing up her *franglaise*, the Jeep has been serviced and a Sea France passage booked.

Nikki Ellen, chatelaine of Crockshard Farm, apparently having pardoned my earlier outrageous observations, is content to allow us to darken her doors again. There is however just a little uncertainty at Orchard House as regards the Guys' unpredictable reaction when faced with Basil her autocratic cat. I resolve to try harder with the door this time. There is another small matter of some import that must be addressed before we revisit Crockshard Farm. This concerns the reaction of the youngest and *après* our earlier encounter, much maligned, daughter of the house. My minor misdemeanour must be addressed before our next meeting. I suspect I'll be forgiven but shall take flowers and chocolates just in case.

Once bitten, we've decided to spend a short week in Haute-Normandie, in a village just outside Dieppe, on our way back. There we'll be able to arrange the obligatory Tick and Tapeworm treatments for the Guys before returning to the UK - anyway we want to see the Bayeux Tapestry and explore some of the D Day battlefields whilst in the area.

On the subject of predicting and hopefully preventing avoidable calamities, I've even booked a table at the Griffin's Head just in case.

We think that we'll be able to drive for longer between the cottages this time so only need one Logis stop and intend to pause just off the *autoroute* at Dijon on our way down to Provence. As it happens our preferred hotel is discovered to be fully booked and 'There being no room at the inn', we've decided to give the Auberge des Trois Jumeaux at Saints-Geosmes another chance. It's roughly in the same area so won't upset the travel arrangements over much. This time I'll try the veal!

On friendship

Our friends have been hugely enthusiastic over our plans and thank goodness for it, otherwise our almost out of date passports might not have been spotted before the off.

We first met when our small estate was new, not entirely complete, strewn with builders' rubble and partly buried in debris; the sort of detritus generally associated with construction sites. Neighbours close at hand, those fortunates whose houses were actually finished and occupied, had volunteered to assist shifting the several large lorry loads of topsoil purchased at no small expense to terrace the inundated unlandscaped precipice that was our friends' embryonic garden.

Our immediate neighbours - the friends who later moved to Spain and whom we visited after Darcey had died - were, like us, ex-army types and doggy folk to boot. Skilled in digging muddy holes in muddy parts of Germany for a living, Himself and Our Hero were obvious candidates for barrowing the earth from its dump at the front along planks to the rear of the house. Sisyphus would have been proud of our efforts that day.

In the driveway of our friends' property where the soil had been unloaded, the lady of the house was much in evidence, conducting operations and generally directing affairs. From a position of advantage at the summit of the muddy mound, she was imprudent enough to attempt close supervision of the hardly inexperienced, unpaid helpers. Thus, while her back was turned, she was vulnerable to the *gentlest* of nudges. Base over apex in the mud, her disreputable, once red anorak even muddier and more disgraceful than before, this good Catholic girl was heard to say a naughty word!

Oh happy days - faced with similar problems the gang all rallied round and much community spirit was generated. Parties at the least excuse; communal litter wombling; skill and tool sharing; simply looking out for each other, these were all the norm. Of course that was some years ago. Now and over time, as the estate has matured and folk have come and gone The Originals, often in the face of vaguely disappointing apathy, try hard to keep the old ways alive.

This is the longest we've ever lived in one place and even though we were seriously considering and actively planning to move to France, we've but recently changed our home ownership strategy from Investing to Nesting and will hopefully see out the evening of our years from the comfort of Orchard House.

149

According to local intelligence, another of our friends - the lady from the walking gang who kindly provided the hotel listing before our last trip to France with Darcey - has been making intimidating noises. She is intolerable adept in matters DIY mainly relating to perpetual house painting; rather like maintaining the Forth Bridge.

There have been dark threats to give Orchard House a television style makeover while we linger abroad. Once her cunning plan was accidentally revealed over tea at our friends' house, I attempted to deflect interest by suggesting flock wallpaper and a trio of china ducks. One can only hope she's joking.

We leave in five days; I must remember to put out the bins.

Chapter Six

Istres Provence

Overture

This morning we were up uncommonly early to glory in a cloudless Mediterranean dawn. Viewed through the stark black silhouettes of our cottage's pine trees and olive grove, the faint radiance, inching above a dark and misted far shore, tints the sky with a deliciously luminous *rosé* glow before gently maturing to a Côtes du Rhône *rouge* and shortly a majestic blaze of brilliant gold - all silently reflected in the calm waters of the Étang de Berre far below us. Sitting with the Guys as the welcome southern sun gradually creeps over the vague skyline of Marseilles far away to the south-east across this immense lagoon, England's lingering snow, slush and freezing rain are far behind us and we feel much the better for it.

Provence seems to have a lyrical effect on me.

Faugh a Ballagh!
Clear the way!

Gaelic

Our latest journey down to the south of France was not entirely uneventful. We left Orchard House about lunchtime on Saturday so the English motorways were largely clear of the foreign motorized thuggery we'd anticipated and frankly its absence was not disagreeable. I venture that the absent heavy goods drivers are probably indulging their self-centred passions at football matches, comparing tattoos and - rather like the *Routiers*, their brutal medieval forebears - hurling foul abuse at the referee. My wife and the dogs have no opinion on the matter.

Later in Kent, Crockshard Farm was much as ever. Following our last stay and its subsequent scurrilous observations, my offence seems spent and I appear to have been rehabilitated. Perhaps the chocolates helped? We didn't care to leave the Guys for too long, after all they're youngsters yet, so we gave a lengthy supper at the Griffin's Head a miss opting instead for a rather nice though shorter, baguette and drink in a welcoming nearby village pub. Rural Kent it seems, is well blessed with many such convivial establishments; this is clearly a matter that requires further investigation.

Next morning we managed to avoid further contempt from the cat Basil by leaving at some ungodly pre-dawn hour, well before anyone else was up and doing, so as to catch a very early Sea France sailing from Dover. A coffee and *croissant* breakfast on board will make a reasonable substitute for Crockshard's tea and toast.

Packing our overnight things and loading the Guys into their travelling cage, I observed that the Jeep, for all its additional capacity, seemed somewhat full but my wife is officer-in-charge of such matters and I find it prudent to remember that at all times. On reflection and with the benefit of long redundant academic business qualifications, I think, rather like Parkinson's Law, that it's a matter of luggage expanding to fill all the available space, which is as good a paradigm as any.

The weather forecasts we consulted before leaving home predicted storms both on the continent and in the Channel but our ferry, stately as a galleon and resolute in the teeth of gale force winds, was largely unmoved by such trivia arriving in Calais spot on time.

Before much longer, on the *autoroute* south, things came to a very different pass as the intemperate conditions worsened, becoming increasingly tempestuous and creating significant obstacles to progress. Although buffeted by fierce side winds, our tough but hardly aerodynamic, Jeep coped manfully with the lashing rain and spray. Just to add to the nuisance, the carriageway was repeatedly carpeted in parts with a deep layer of debris stripped from roadside trees and this needed careful navigation, especially round the bigger branches, so as to avoid the obvious danger to life, limb and bodywork. Having lost not too much time, it was something of a relief eventually to reach St Geosmes and the welcoming embrace of Logis de France, only to find more misery awaiting us there. Once again *Monsieur* is *désolé*. The *auberge's* restaurant is closed on Sunday nights. *Post hoc* it seems that the veal is to be denied me.

Almost predictably, *ergo propter hoc,* nearby Langres

153

annoyingly shuts up shop on the Sabbath. All is closed for the duration, dead to the world, silent as the grave and apart from a handy cash machine, nothing stirs. Now in funds, the officer-in-charge messing and accommodation has expressed her will and must eat, and I find it prudent...etc. In and among the township's archaic religious torpor, a heretical refuge in the form of a brightly lit McDonald's fast food eatery shines like a beacon in the gloom and is obviously predestined to come to the rescue. This is a first for us and being unsure of the rules, we novices enter with some trepidation. Appropriately enough, the bright modern restaurant is found to be in apple pie order and insufferably hygienic. Wedged tightly into vibrant plastic furniture, surrounded by brash, brightly illuminated, menus and attended by a host of juvenile extras who all know the script, Big Mac provides us with an instantaneous chicken, bacon and onion filled bun. Truth be told, this is rather good - perhaps it's because I'm hungry? Possibly I'm out of date and somewhat old fashioned, but for all that I rather enjoyed the fast food, I much prefer my restaurants understated and candlelit; the *maitre d'* grand; the waiters deferential and grateful for the tip; and above all, to have room to swing a cat.

Next morning having managed the Sleep of the Just and the *auberge's* decent *café crème* and *croissant* breakfast, the five hour run down the Rhône valley to the small town of Istres was largely uneventful and a comparatively more pleasant experience. The damaging *Vents latéral violent* having abated somewhat, the Jeep took the bit firmly between its teeth, ploughing on south while the Guys, shades of Darcey Bussell, spent the trip soundly asleep in the back.

154

Le petit mas de l'Aupière

Après midi. Nous sommes arrivés! …and our first cottage is simply delightful. Situated in woodland on the south eastern heights of the isthmus separating the Étang de l'Olivier from the much larger Étang de Berre, it is not quite blighted by national grid electricity pylons and occasional uproar from a military airbase within distant earshot. Connected to the owners' house by a covered walkway, Le petit mas de l'Aupière is built on one level in a vaguely Romanesque style. We have taken the property for a month and after a couple of false starts, are greeted and shown round by our hostess. *Madame* is an attractive tall blond, much younger than expected, who, unconsciously flaunting much *chic*, looks incredibly healthy in the Mediterranean sunshine and, contrary to the modern trend, is possessed of incredibly limited English. Exchanging obligatory kisses (*'Trois fois en Provence!'*) I immediately forgive her all these minor shortcomings and am promptly taken firmly in hand by the officer-in-charge translation and discipline.

Moving in is but a minor travail involving much baggage handling by me and a great deal of organising by the officer-in-charge until, *étonnement!* We've finished. Both the house and Jeep, by now configured for touring, are tidy and ordered and refreshments may be taken. Relaxing on our sunny south facing stone veranda with glass in hand, we ring our friends to enjoy a cheap gloat. As a treat and much influenced by a heavy 'Bums on beds' discount, they, like us, spent Sunday night away but their accommodation was a travel motel just off the M6 motorway in dismal Wigan; a place where English is allegedly spoken. Today they planned to motor over to

155

sunny Southport for a leisurely weekday promenade and shopping expedition. Genteel Edwardian Southport is a regular outing for them and a lunch destination they much enjoy. Oh joy! There was a hailstorm.

Providing they can benefit from last minute low cost flights, our friends have threatened to join us for a couple of days when we reach the Dordogne; planning to stay at Eymet in the same B&B we shared on our excursion *après* dear old Darcey's sad end. This would be nice and we'll hear more from them later no doubt. I've counselled against a short trip unless the price is a not to be missed offer but they'll make up their own minds on what's an acceptable fare. I hope they can make it.

彤 彤

Le petit mas de l'Aupière is a very Mediterranean affair with few concessions to chilly wet days and its *en suite* bathroom is similarly ordered. Cold or warm it would be a delight but for the substantial interconnecting door which opens inward. Whatever I try I simply cannot enter the bathroom without stepping into the shower cubicle in order to close it. It's rather analogous to Poe's *The Pit and the Pendulum*. The officer-in-charge was heard to be humming the *Rocky Horror Picture Show's* '*It's just a jump to the left…*' as I made for my ablutions this morning. Odd sense of humour my wife.

As it's on the edge of woodlands the Little Farm's garden is well fenced and in places this barrier is complemented with a battery driven electric stock ribbon. Sometimes situated within the boundary and occasionally without, I wondered about its purpose but have decided that it's there to keep larger wild fauna out. Elle decided that this morning would be a good time to investigate its mysteries. The yelp as her inquisitive wet nose touched the cable almost drowned out the local air force's din. Bless!

Étang d' Berre

Getting one's bearings is a must. Within a couple of days of arrival we've charted Istres and nearby Miramas, so today we'll circumnavigate the Étang d' Berre. Apparently, as well as being a famed wildlife sanctuary, there's a lot of modern history wrapped up in its waters so it will be fun driving round the shoreline to spot the various locations identified in our Under Fives' guide book. The massive lagoon figures in French military aeronautics having once been a training school for naval seaplane pilots - it seems that salt water was an important factor for primitive and underpowered float-planes' performance and buoyancy. With the demise of such antiquated naval aviation there are a number of huge redundant hangers still to be seen, one of which has been converted into a massive municipal indoor swimming pool, *La piscine* Claude Jouve. Nowadays the *étang* serves as an aquatic filling station for the *Pompiers'* amphibious fire fighting Canadair aircraft from which, without landing, they scoop water to dump onto Provence's frequent forest fires.

Situated on the eastern shore there are huge, rather intrusive, oil refineries to be negotiated before one becomes entangled in the *autoroute* bedlam that is the hinterland of Marseilles' busy Marignane airport that juts out into the water of the *étang's* south-eastern corner.

Once clear of the motorway's chaos we soon arrive at Martigues where there is a narrow waterway giving access to the Mediterranean's Golfe de Fos. Glimpsed from the heights of the carriageway, the old town and waterway below look enchanting and we are determined to visit in a quieter weekday moment.

Returning to Istres we rate our expedition good in parts, especially the lakeside villages where we managed to spot much birdlife including some flamingos. The motorways around Marignane were the usual bore but at Saint-Chamas the ancient Roman *Pont Flavian* bridge and road, with its preserved chariot rutted surface, more than confirmed the enduring need for such means of travel facilitating communications, commerce and of course, conflict.

🐕 🐕

Wrangler owners tend to eschew roads but there's a lot to be said for a trundle in the Jeep down to the supermarket, driving in glorious sunshine with the front roof panels removed. Although I have sunglasses to hand I venture that I might need to buy a baseball cap to help to reduce the fierce overhead glare. My wife thinks I'm far too old for such foolishness so I get my own back by blasting forth outdated ABBA tunes for the benefit of passing cars and innocent pedestrians.

At a nearby school 6th form traffic monitors, the sensible French equivalents of the UK's lollipop attendants, are stopping passing traffic to sell souvenirs for a local children's charity. In the spirit of *fraternité* and because we favour such charitable enterprise, the Jeep now boasts a magnificent tricolour.

I've noticed that unlike the Saab, our new Jeep tends to promote anti-Flocking behaviour on the car parks in and around Istres. We are given a wide berth wherever we stop. Based on as yet empirical and fairly local evidence, this tends to support our purchasing decision and bodes well for the future. I'm thinking of submitting a short dissertation on the subject.

Lubéron encore

It's sunny and the sky is a cloudless blue but there is a fierce gale blowing, so this morning my wife decided that a return visit to the Lubéron might make a nice outing. The TomTom GPS ensured that the drive north was *interesting* until we managed to access the motorway at Lançon. Turning east at Cavaillon, Mount Ventoux and the hills to the north were snow covered but in the valley the clear weather was mild and relatively wind free. High in the village of Bonnieux a delicious *café crème* made a nice break before we reversed course and made a leisurely return to Istres. Although, due to unfortunately intrusive publicity, he's now moved on, Peter Mayle's valley really is stunningly beautiful.

Later, taking it easy on our still windy veranda, I sampled a slice of *terrine d' Porc,* which was an impulse purchase on our way home. Irrespective of the breeze the rough pork *pâté* with a glass of *vin rouge* makes a delicious full stop to a nice *ad hoc* day. I just had to have a mobile phone gloat with our friends to discover they've been tracking our local weather via the Internet. He thinks we're suffering a severe case of the Mistral. I said we really didn't care and just to reinforce the point chatted to his wife instead. Apparently there's been an issue with the keys they have to gain access to Orchard House. They've promised to keep a gentle eye our mail but couldn't gain entry. Thank goodness the lady of the house has resolved matters.

🐕 🐕

We once owned a Citroën 2CV *deux chevaux* an unconventional vehicle, which I bought as a cheap utilitarian means of commuting for which it made an ideal, if somewhat eccentric, choice. Among its several irritating features was the pathetic fondness for an obligatory acknowledging wave from other unfortunate owners when passing. In the Lubéron and again this morning we encountered Wranglers coming in the opposite direction. I waved and flashed our headlights and so did the other pair of Jeep drivers. Good grief!

Déjeuner de dimanche

Because we're staying longer at our various destinations this time, somewhat arbitrarily I've decided that we shall make a real effort to eat out at the weekends. The officer-in-charge messing and accommodation has concurred but this rather grey and damp morning we lingered abed, consequently tea and toast were taken late and a planned outing to a nearby restaurant for Sunday lunch was delayed. An hour or so later I contrived to return to Le petite mas via our preferred dining choice, by which time lunch was back on.

The small restaurant is not quite out of town and a family affair. I know this because *Mademoiselle*, very stylish, very pretty and very assured, is all of eight years

160

old. However, age not withstanding, front of house matters are well in hand; with only occasional assistance being required from *Maman* who is largely occupied assisting *Papa dans la cuisine* when not otherwise employed delivering the hotter dishes to table. Our order is taken with but the merest of linguistic disruption and just a little assistance from *Maman* regarding the availability of our preferred wine. Fresh bread is sliced with a confident air and served with home-made black *provençal tapanade*, which is delicious. I have seconds. Our respective starters of smoked salmon on toast and carpaccio of beef are quite excellent and we have no hesitation in confirming this to *Mademoiselle's* confident: *'Etait ce bon?'* enquiry as she cleared the plates and cutlery. After delicious beef steak and breast of roast *canard* have been demolished and in a gesture of affectionate *fraternité*, during the cheese and pudding courses I embark on some light English lessons and soon *Mademoiselle* can report to *Maman et Papa* that *l'anglais* rated their lunch: 'Vairry gude.' Her ten-year-old brother, not yet trusted with customers, is unimpressed.

Coffee taken, the bill is a trivial matter but before money can change hands, *Papa*, still aglow from the ovens, insists we sample his home brewed *digestif*, a clear fiery spirit that is poured furtively from a recycled plastic water bottle. A small measure of the powerful aromatic liqueur damn near brings tears to my eyes while cleaning my teeth as well as my palate. This rite of passage successfully negotiated our account, including a modest gratuity for the children, is settled and *'Au revoir jusqu'à la prochaine fois'* we part firm friends.

Mistral!

Will she never learn? Elle has just suffered another shocking encounter with the electric stock fence. Sam on the other hand seems to have benefited from Elle's experience and keeps well away from the live wire. Clever boy!

🐕 🐕

During the protracted business of obtaining the Guys' pet passports, our local vet had horror stories to share regarding various maladies that can afflict small dogs when *en vacance* on the Mediterranean's warm and sandy shores. Even though we are abroad in the lowest of low season, on his strong recommendation they have been temporarily equipped with additional anti flea collars and hatefully subjected to extra tick treatments, all at no little expense. Elle has recently been found to be scratching which is unusual and worrying until it's discovered that companionable rough and tumbling have damn near destroyed the lining of her collar and this is now irritating her neck. A similar thing happened to Sam in their earlier days together so we're fairly certain that this is the problem rather than some dire foreign infestation. Fortunately we've spotted a pets' supermarket on the road to Martigues where we'll be able to buy a replacement, which no doubt she'll hate.

🐕 🐕

The Mistral is upon us. The Lubéron, Nimes, Arles and Avignon are all snowbound. According to the local newspaper, La Provence (*so it must be true*) there is a tailback of four thousand *camions* stuck on the motorway near Arles. The stranded HGV drivers do not merit my sympathy. Here it's a bright sunny day but the wind is gusting at storm velocity and the temperature has dropped like a stone. Buried among its typically parochial stories La Provence is forecasting much better conditions for the weekend. In the meantime in our quest for a new collar for Elle, we took the opportunity to visit Martigues as we'd promised ourselves we would.

Although it's very pretty Martigues hardly ranks among France's larger towns. I mention this because small though it may be, Our Hero became hopelessly trapped in the wrong traffic lane while attempting to gain the clearly marked *Centre Ville*. After another *interesting* detour, eventually we left the modern town *Toutes directions* to discover the old town and port as charming as we'd hoped. A closer pedestrian inspection will have to wait until the freezing weather improves considerably. On our way back to Istres we took the opportunity to explore a sign posted beach which just took our fancy, and our impromptu trip to the *plage* became a rather nice countryside excursion as we meandered our way back towards Martigues through some ideal dog walking countryside. This is an excellent and fortunate discovery as there aren't many locations available to exercise the Guys near our cottage.

Later we drove out to Saint Martin de Crau where there is to be a *Qinquantenaire* festival next week, which we plan to visit. A grand parade graced by *Les Gardians*, the Camargue's mounted herdsmen, is planned with a livestock show featuring the area's native bulls to follow. This should be great fun and we hope the weather will improve for the occasion.

Having too quickly disparaged the dog walking facilities in and around Le petit mas de l'Aupière, my wife has this very morning discovered a somewhat obscure track giving reasonably easy access to the nearby woods; something I've clearly overlooked when out with the Guys. This is excellent news and although the weather is still bitterly cold and blustery, we wrap up warmly and waste no time in exploring the *bois*. Although the mixed woodland is largely unmanaged, the terrain is heavily terraced with many rocky outcrops and is dotted here and there with rather bijou but considering the setting, not entirely inappropriate dwellings that comprise both weekend retreats and permanent residences. These are to be found mainly on the heights and woodland margins where they are carefully sited to take advantage of the spectacular lagoon views.

Our track wandered its way north on the spine of the peninsula until progress was unexpectedly halted, rather unreasonably to my mind, by an unsightly gate and disagreeable fences. These try hard to retain a seedy enclosure containing several down-at-heel stalls, sties and cages but no livestock. We being guests in the country the idea of burglary in order to advance progress did not seem entirely appropriate, nor it might be added, could we guess what ghastly canine contagion lurked within, so in the absence of a ready to hand alternative path we gently wended our way back to the cottage. *En route* and much to the Guys' chagrin, the officer-in-charge implemented some recently neglected obedience training. After some mild indiscipline they soon settled down but observing their excitable demeanour in this new environment, I despair that we'll ever be able to allow them off their leads safely. Nevertheless our walk made a charming detour, one that we shall take care to investigate at more length as our stay here progresses.

🐕 🐕

We had a visit from our host last evening. He seems a nice chap and amid an uproar of greeting from the Guys, there were times when we almost understood what he was trying to tell us. It seems there is to be a Saint Patrick's festival on the 19th of March, which, as far as we could establish, is quite an occasion hereabouts. I rather suspect it's all a clever ploy to enjoy a thoroughly secular late Lent rave up; an ingenious means of breaking the season's customary fast without sullying religious correctness over much. He's asked if we'd like tickets for the event. *Naturellement!*

Monsieur came armed with gifts of crisp fresh lettuce and better still, a bottle of olive oil pressed from their own crop. Afterwards we tried some on a rip of fresh bread. It was absolutely delicious. I feel rather guilty that, caught on the hop with the dogs adding to the chaos, I didn't have the wit to offer him a drink. No doubt there'll be other opportunities.

Today's a brilliantly sunny day and but for the glacial temperature and furious winds we'd be sunbathing. Walking the Guys on our new trail this morning the puddles were icy. Ah! The lure of the Mediterranean. Last night *Monsieur* was wreathed in apologies for the Mistral, no doubt thinking that our visit was ruined. He's yet to learn that *l'anglais* are made of sterner stuff.

It's still much too snowbound for travel north so we've been confining ourselves to trips about the immediate area. Even then it's very cold and blustery but on a

165

return visit to Martigues we found a sun trapped waterfront cafe where, almost sheltered from the Mistral's icy grips, we watched the yachts and passing traffic but not quite in shirtsleeves. Later I was interested to observe the town's heroic efforts to combat the blankets of dense green algae that are prone to blight the shoreline hereabouts. *Monsieur* drives his tractor deep into the surf towing a contraption much like a low-level combined harvester. This invention not only gathers in the offending accumulation but bails it ready to be deposited into a waiting skip. Apart from the stench, an interesting process - one that I shall cherish.

La Provence has promised improvements for next week so Arles and Nîmes look fair for exploration followed by our much anticipated return to Avignon. In the interim there's the festival at Saint Martin de Crau to look forward to.

🐕 🐕

Le weekend and the Mistral has almost abated. Le petit mas de l'Aupière is a south facing suntrap so we are relishing the gorgeous weather; a brilliant cloudless Mediterranean sky with glorious sunshine is our current lot and we're much pleased with it. After a quick shop and a *croque M'sieur* snack at the supermarket we spend the afternoon at home in the garden with the Guys, relishing the weather and watching others work.

The garden's olive trees are being pruned. Although not quite a labour of Hercules nevertheless it's a daunting task requiring care and judgement. Throughout a long day the gardener has stuck to his task so that at least half of the orchard has been trimmed. Shorn of excess unruly growth their bare gnarled trunks now support close cropped unnatural crowns, rather like arboreal crew cuts. Our host, who is clearly very proud of his trees and their produce, explained that some of the trees are quite old. I would have liked to have described the ancient olives we saw at Le Thoronet Abbey where some have been trained around walls of stone blocks cemented within their boles and trunks, but even with our excellent translation software, the task was beyond me.

Without any effort I did manage to force a drink on him this time.

It's a strange thing but wherever we stay, there's always something in the cottages to be discovered but often too late to be of any use. For example, at Le Beausset a couple of years ago we simply could not turn on the living room's overhead reading lamps. It was only on our very last day when, completely by accident, we discovered their switches tucked away behind the built in settees' fitted cushions.   Grief!

Yesterday was a day of discovery at the Little Farm. As usual on our arrival my wife made sensible accommodation arrangements for various necessities such as dog leads, walking boots, grub and booze etc., much as you've now come to expect from the officer-in-charge of these matters.   Our heavy dog walking anoraks, much needed in the recent freezing conditions, were assigned to a completely inadequate and rather rusty nail in the utilities cupboard - a far from satisfactory arrangement. On an adjacent wall, just where you'd expect coat hooks to be positioned, is to be seen a substantial lath of silk varnished warm teak.   Placed horizontally it has equidistant flush fitted polished metal strips let vertically into its surface.   At first glance a piece of unconvincing modern art.   Quite by chance I've discovered that it has a hidden *raison d'être*.   The strips unfold.   *Voila!*   The coat hanger.

Similarly, on a well founded principle of 'When all else fails - read the instructions.'   (...*or more usually in Orchard House; 'Destructions'*) we have unexpectedly managed to connect to the Interweb.   As usual when on holiday abroad we've not bothered with television but quite by chance during a snoop of the cottage's amenities, I discovered an odd piece of computer hardware lurking in the TV set's cabinet and a strange Internet code scribbled on the front page of a compendium of instructions for the household's equipment.   Once connected the Laptop downloaded blasted emails for hours and as usual none of the messages mattered a damn but we did manage to check the Lotto results.   Surprise, surprise we've not won a million!

Out and about on a pleasant Sunday

This morning we were up and about early for the much-anticipated St Martin De Crau festival. It starts at 11:00 am and the drive over will take a little over half an hour so I struggle awake ahead of myself and walk the Guys at a gallop. Ablutions and walking completed we set off in brilliant sunshine. In the countryside the wind is still gusty but we make good time and manage to arrive with half an hour or so in hand. On arrival the village shows absolutely no signs of festival or festivities and after a couple of passes along the main street, all we have observed is the normal cafe activity one expects on a fine Sunday morning in France. Uncertain if we've wasted our time we join the convention and settle for a consolation brace of *café crème* in a clearly popular *centre ville* cafe. Coffee taken and no parade in sight we decide to call it a day and returning to the Jeep, head for home. Not quite in the outskirts while pausing for traffic, I notice a local *gendarme* patrol car in a quiet side street with its blue emergency lights flashing and before long observe it in my rear view mirror emerging into the main thoroughfare now leading the municipal band. Not to be defeated it takes but a moment to reverse course, park and gain a reasonable reviewing position.

The Saint Martin De Crau Grand *Qinquantenaire* Parade comprises: the *gendarme*s in their car; the scarlet-coated band; some majorettes; a dozen or so pedestrians in local costume; and *Les Gardians*. Mounted three by three with younger participants protected in the centre rank, some thirty or so of the Camargue's finest, astride their creamy horses and dressed in traditional garb, pass in review. Armed with fearsome eight foot long, trefoil tipped lances they make a fine sight while dropping horse dung liberally underhoof. With the band contributing a good deal of noise and the *gendarme*s a lot less light, they pass by our but recently vacated prime cafe position and are gone in mere minutes. The cattle show starts in three and a half hours time at 2:30 pm, shall we stay? Perhaps not!

The leisurely drive back to Istres is interrupted only by a less formal livestock show of our own when we encounter a massive flock of bell equipped but, in comparison with our own Pennine varieties, disappointingly off-white sheep. Taking advantage of a quiet Sunday they are being driven along the highway by their shepherds and, what I took to be, their local Briard sheepdogs. Monopolizing the nearside carriageway, cycle path and most of the huge drainage ditch, the huge flock is remarkably composed, well in hand and in but a moment, *Monsieur* cheerfully waves us on, so we pass by on the other side.

We've been pondering a wall. Between Istres and Miramas on the way to Saint Martin De Crau there is a substantial edifice of concrete posts and sections of the sort that provides instant garden walling - but much, much larger. This enormous, patently expensive structure, that seems to stretch for miles and protects nothing obvious, has intrigued us every time we've passed by. Could it be part of the French air force's nuclear airbase; something to do with the Space Shuttle's emergency landing facilities; a high security prison? Nothing so exciting: I've recently discovered that this was the once famous but now redundant, Miramas racing circuit and is currently the home of the BMW car firm's testing track. What a bore.

The morning all but gone we forgo a planned lunch and taking full advantage of the glorious weather strip the roof panels from the Jeep and drive out to Saint-Chamas for a closer inspection of its remarkably well preserved Roman bridge. This gives me a first chance to sport my baseball cap, newly acquired for just such eventualities. I ignore much derision from the cheap seats.

I'm the photographer in the family but my wife has caught the bug. As a result, a year or so ago I bought her a not quite expensive pocket camera, which she promptly used at the least excuse, snapping away like a woman possessed. Given its limitations it must be admitted that some of her work is quite good. Preparing for this trip the camera could not be found. After much house and soul searching it was eventually declared lost or stolen and I treated her to a much better replacement as a combined birthday and anniversary treat.

Retrieving the travelling bags from the loft before packing for our journey, the missing camera was discovered lurking within one of them, clearly left there forgotten after our last break. I did not gloat nor did I criticise, so am disappointed, nay saddened, by the recent mocking of my hat.

Crossing the fast flowing river Touloubre in its deep ravine, the ancient *Pont Flavian* does not disappoint. The superb bas-relief imperial eagles, inscriptions and wonderfully sculpted lions atop the tall triumphal arch's still crisp columns, remain a fine testament to its builders' skill. Some of the construction we frankly did not understand. For example, there are internal hump backed ramps acting much like a chicane at each side of the bridge's apex with almost square sockets carved deep into their surfaces. I imagine it's an ancient single file traffic arrangement but can't quite reconcile the crossing's obvious strength and staying power with the necessity for such measures nor yet grasp what the sockets were intended for.

The bridge inspected and admired, we return to Istres and by the merest of happy coincidences, almost pass by the family restaurant where we dined recently …and it's not too late for Sunday lunch. We succumb.

Picture this

Today has been an extravagance. I lay abed disgracefully late while my wife saw to the Guys and carried out routine housekeeping and light maintenance. Later, lazing in the afternoon's sunshine over a glass of *rosé* and more or less engaged in editing earlier musings, I reflected on photographic matters. Last year, pressed for a Christmas gift for The Girl Who Has Everything, I thought it might be a nice idea to commission a painting of the Guys. Courtesy of the Internet, Penny Richardson of Leicestershire came up trumps and her painting, captured from a couple of my wife's Bamburgh snapshots, now adorns our sitting room. Situated not quite in pride of place beside an earlier portrait of my wife, her results A Rose Between Two Thorns, graces the title page of this book. Quite how I got into the act is another matter.

Not unexpectedly we're members of the UK's

Northern Parson Russell Terrier Club and last year, a fellow member who is much concerned with breed rescues, sought aid in providing amusing Parson Russell pictures to adorn her charitable calendar. Elle, courtesy of my wife's photographic endeavours and head deep in Bamburgh's surf, is now Miss August.

Les Baux de Provence

If you're a connoisseur of aluminium smelting, as I'm sure many of you are, then Les Baux de Provence is a place you simply cannot afford to miss; for this is where its ore's name originates. In the unlikely event that you're not, visit anyway because this medieval township is simply spectacular.

Owing to last night's trivial surfeit of red wine, which rather affected my equilibrium this morning, we walked the Guys a little later than usual and on our way back to the cottage met two charming lady neighbours who felt obliged to practice their English. In the event their efforts proved much better than my *franglaise* and after they had admired the dogs, we fell to discussing our itinerary on which subject they had a couple of additional suggestions to offer. One of these was Les Baux de Provence, home to a Not To Be Missed *château* and Bauxite ore. Since it lies in the mountains not far beyond Saint Martin de Crau we ignored the parlous state of my liver, seized the opportunity, and drove over for an afternoon's sightseeing.

Situated high on the southern aspect of the Alpilles Mountains commanding the alluvial Crau plain of the Bouches du Rhône, Les Baux was an ancient hill fort or *oppidum*. By the early Middle Ages the prosperous Lords of Baux controlled much of the region and unsuccessfully sought to further extend their rule to include the whole of Provence. By the mid 15th century their rule had ended but their legacy lived on in Baux's great castle renowned for its sophistication and as a seat of chivalry. Later, having become a protestant stronghold, Baux led a failed revolt against the crown, which resulted in Cardinal Richelieu ordering the castle's demolition. Hegemony, it seems, was never Baux's strong suit.

In 1642 the town and lordship was gifted to the royal family of Monaco and even though Baux remains stoutly and legally French, the Grimaldi Princess Caroline makes use of its title to this day.

During excavations of 1822 the geologist Pierre Berthier discovered Bauxite nearby which, in the way of all entrepreneurial endeavour and given Baux's woeful track record in such enterprises, was doomed to be mined to exhaustion by the late 20th century.

174

The township and its castle, rated with Carcassonne and the Eiffel Tower as most visited in France, is strikingly pretty in pale stone with steeply rising narrow cobbled streets leading ever up to the ruins of its castle. Well blessed with fine restaurants and much arts and crafts set alongside the inevitable tawdry souvenir shops, unsurprisingly, Baux, its population now measured in dozens, is these days entirely given over to tourism.

It seems that the medieval *chevaliers* of Baux employed a courage enhancing perfume of Cypress before riding into their largely disappointing battles. According to my sources, its recipe still figures in a *provençal* gentlemen's aftershave today. Frankly I could have used a little of their elixir this morning.

Observations on misunderstanding the dangers of red wine

This time I've promised the editor-in-chief not to dwell too much on things past but my recent fragile condition provided just cause to reflect on a case of an excess of red plonk and some slight confusion.

Not long after retiring from the army, having narrowly avoided a final confrontation with the military's often less than compassionate medical services, they finally cornered me. Under pain of future damnation and dire threats to my pension rights, I was urged by registered letter to a non-negotiable alternative examination with a civilian doctor. Early on the prearranged Monday morning, I presented myself to a charming local practitioner who, this being his first exposure to the requirements of Her Majesty and the Army Act, seemed

175

much interested in my circumstances. After some companionable chat during which, having demolished a half decent *vin rouge* the previous evening, I apologised in advance for possibly upsetting his chemical analysis, he took a history. Although normally as fit as a butcher's dog, I felt obliged to own up to a soldier's traditional corporeal damage; wrecked knees and Gunner Ear. Somewhat surprisingly given his previous warmth, the doctor promptly busied himself in papers and his stethoscope but a little later and rather coyly, suggested that it might be a good idea not to mention my social disease in future. Social disease? What was the man thinking? All innocence but not altogether unknowingly, I enquired. Without quite meeting my eye: 'You know; your Gonorrhoea' he mumbled sheepishly. Given my fragile condition and in the circumstances perhaps a little loudly, I explained that rather than possessed of some horrid venereal malady I suffer gunfire deafness. He quickly saw the joke and we laughed like drains. Bless! I understand that he's been dining out on the tale ever since.

A little local sightseeing

Mirimas le Vieux, a mini Baux, figured on today's agenda. It's just across the corner of the *étang* from our cottage and since we didn't want the effort of driving far, seemed a nice local destination.

Another castle dominated *oppidum* we crawled ever upward with the Jeep making no effort at all until we reached the ruins. The problem now lay in the ever-diminishing road width. *Madame* in her Megan raced ahead of us until out of sight and then, horror of horrors, she came back down. Nose to nose she pulled into her allotted parking space just before serious decisions on manoeuvring the unwieldy Jeep were required. Thank goodness for the French lunch.

The views from the ruined *château* were stunning; unfortunately the village was in hibernation so as coffee was clearly off, we dallied only long enough to satisfy my wife's lust for photography before creeping back down inclines that would not disgrace the north face of the Eiger.

St Mitre les Remparts en route to Martigues seemed a sensible second stop. Apart from the potential romance of its name we rated it dull and equally narrow as Miramas le Vieux. I think a little more research is needed before we ever consider a return.

Port de Bouc, the Étang de Berre's uninspiring gateway to the Mediterranean, is appalling and smelled of oil refineries.

Supper of cold cuts and salad dressed with *Monsieur's* olive oil with a delicious glass of red made up for it all. We shall try harder tomorrow.

Not quite bagpipes

Last night was Istres' grand St Patrick's show. Our hosts had kindly obtained a pair of free tickets for us and the performance was due to commence at 7:30 pm. We'd enjoyed a long day's sightseeing so all anticipation and not knowing quite what to expect, we drove down to the venue for 7:00 pm, surely early enough, only to be greeted by the very worst of utter chaos. Thereabouts most of the population of the town was to be found in a positive blood lust of car parking anarchy, everyone fighting over completely inadequate space around the concert hall. By the time the show was due to start and still wrestling with the unwieldy Jeep among the other unfortunates, we'd used about a quarter of a tank of diesel and all of my patience. Carlos Núñez, his frenetic Galician bagpipes and the rest of the boys in the band will just have to wait for another opportunity to entertain us.

Up-market supper in town, where the parking was only marginally easier, was our consolation prize and if I'm any judge, a much better and probably much quieter deal. Whilst dining we formed the distinct impression that our elegant restaurant was progressively being filled to bursting by our erstwhile and similarly disenchanted competitors. For a not quite unreasonable bill the food was exceptional, the service excellent and an outstanding claret neatly rounded off the experience.

Fortunately for us I rather fancy that our hosts won't be able to summon up the language to ask if we enjoyed the show. We shall keep quiet but buy a large bunch of thank you flowers for *Madame*.

Van Gogh, the Romans and some Jack Russell puppies

For all that his paintings command millions I've never quite been able to class myself as a member of poor mad Vincent Van Gogh's huge fan club. Arles, famous as one of his last abodes shortly before being packed off to the lunatic asylum, figured prominently as the setting of many of his finest paintings.

A common enough mixture of the ancient, medieval, modern and downright scruffy, Arles is typical of many of the towns founded as resettlement colonies for veterans of the Roman legions to be found scattered on the trade routes between Italy and Spain and beyond. Today's Arles boasts a very fine and well preserved Roman amphitheatre, albeit one overlain with medieval additions and questionable modern preservation. Together with a nearby ancient theatre, triumphal arch and defensive walls it lends more than a little depth and texture to Arles' colourful picture. The historic stadium is still in use even now and as we took time to inspect its various merits, the arena, long devoid of brutal gladiators, was being prepared for a similarly belligerent bullfight to take place later this month.

179

We spend our morning among the Romans and numerous tourists both ancient and modern, before taking a leisurely lunch in a positively antique street cafe. I loved the faintly archaic look of the place; a more or less traffic free, narrow paved lane all overhung with venerable electric street lights and rather unlikely attempts at medieval guild signs. *Madame's* lunch with a refreshing glass of cold beer was a much needed restorative before the bell for the commencement of round two with Vincent and Julius Ceasar.

Later and by now walked to ground idle, we strolled past a pet shop where within its windows, basking in air-conditioned sunshine, Jack Russell puppies were on show. Though we were replete from lunch they looked good enough to eat but not to buy and clearly not in the Guys' league. We pass on.

Camargue

Some years ago we lived for a time in East Anglia. In hindsight and rather rashly, then and afterwards, I tended to mock its inhabitants as Flat Earthers. Almost a race apart, their vast levels, fens, huge skies and a comparatively languid pace of life were unfamiliar, perhaps uncomfortable, experiences for this temporary interloper in their domains. Mind you the fenlanders themselves didn't do much to help. In a small community centred about pub and parish, we lived and played our part in village life for five long years before gaining but a minor measure of rather awkward acceptance. Neither unkind nor uncaring *chacun à son goût,* they just had their own and to us rather unfamiliar, way of going about life.

The Camargue strikes me as very similar. It consists of an extensive alluvial wetland, its silted marshy plains contained within an almost right angled triangle nestling between the arms of the Rhône after it divides above Arles into the Petite Rhône to the west and the easterly Grand Rhône. It is dominated by the Étang de Vaccarès, a vast shallow brine lagoon, whose solitary dunes border the Mediterranean to the south where they form a spectacular hypotenuse.

Famous for its indigenous white horses and an incredible catalogue of wildlife the Camargue is a lonely wild strikingly beautiful, marshland.

We enter from ghastly Port du Bouc with its malodorous refineries and an obligatory rank of horrid wind turbines, by way of a diminutive local ferry service over the Grand Rhône.   Aboard for a mere ten-minute voyage, notices in French and English demand that the Jeep's engine be switched off and the hand brake applied. At least that's what we understood 'Grip the handbrake' to be suggesting; so, emulating the late Michael Flanders when challenged with unintelligible airport announcements: 'We did that!'

Once ashore, Salin de Giraud is Bournville chocolate's altruistic equivalent of salt production but in miniature and in France. With its orderly rows of workers' cottages but a complete absence of folk, already there is a sense of change.   The pace is slower and marked by an absence of the frenetic French traffic but a river's width and a world away.

Our plan is to circumnavigate the Étang de Vaccarès

using convenient byways and side roads. We'll journey anti clockwise around the lagoon ending our trip at Saintes Maries de la Mere and thank goodness for the robust Jeep. The Saab would have proved much too dainty for the meandering, rough and very bumpy rural lanes we found ourselves negotiating.

The Camargue is an isolated haven of managed wetlands with many dykes and watercourses, organised to preserve its otherwise transient, alluvial character. There are ubiquitous stands of towering dun coloured reed beds to be found alongside the numerous ditches and waterways where many species of aquatic plants flourish. As we pass we see many rafts of irises, not yet in flower but surely a wonderful show for later spring visitors. Irregular lines of mixed woodland trees - which add essential stability for the soil, windbreaks and cover for the area's famed birdlife - mark the way. Interspersed with many rather muddy brine pools of various sizes, incredible arrays of birds are evident and as we putter along we see many egrets, flamingos and omnipresent common waterfowl. At one point we disturb a magnificent buzzard, which lazily glides away ahead of us before setting down once more to the solitary vigilance of its hunt.

Much like Hampshire's New Forest ponies, there are many of the Camargue's white horses at large, as well as some well-fenced pastures containing the area's equally famous black bulls. Viewed from a distance and for the moment apparently docile, these animals are bred to fight in the ring and happily are, for the moment, safely confined.

Later on the road south we pass a junction leading off

to La Petite Camargue's Aigues Mortes. (*Dead Waters*) Once a thriving port but now situated five kilometres inland, it more than serves to illustrate the Camargue's ephemeral earlier character.

At Les Saintes Maries de la Mere we experience a sense of *déjà vu*; this seaside town could be a slightly less vibrant Narbonne Plage but possessed of much more character and a lot less sand. We are able to park easily and before exploring take a well deserved sandwich lunch at a nearby esplanade cafe. In keeping with our recent experience at Langres, a steak and chips filled baguette with delicious mayonnaise dressing is another first and whilst rather unusual to be found in a bun, is excellent and absolutely delicious. Sitting in the sunshine with a glass of chilled *rosé* it's clear to me that all's well with the world.

The town's surfeit of Maries derive from the legend of the women of Christ's crucifixion and resurrection - the Myrrh Bearers, Mary Magdalene, Mary Salome and Mary Jacobe - who with Joseph of Arimathea, made their way to France during the persecution of Christians in the first century AD. The story has it that they were accompanied by Saint Sarah, sometime maidservant, occasionally - at least in the French version - Mary Magdalene's daughter, who is now venerated as patroness of the Roma gypsy folk and incredibly, of tattoos and piercing. Quite why she should be the approved benefactress of the latter pair of doubtful decorative customs remains shrouded in mystery. The town's fortified church, a sensible defence against invasion and pillage by various Vikings, Saracens and rapacious pirates, contains her shrine together with silver sheathed 15th century relics allegedly of the Maries Salome and Jacobe. Rather like the veritable forest of fragments of the True Cross, a slightly ambiguous Shroud of Turin is also to be seen in the nave. Saint Sarah's dark skinned, ornately clothed and tiara bedecked statuette is to be found in the crypt from where it is carried in procession to the sea each year during her May time festival.

After an obligatory remembrance candle has been lit and a commemorative medal bought for our friends, we process in turn to view the usual seaside attractions before making for the Jeep and heading for home.

It's been a great day out and we decide to indulge in an encore before we leave for Aquitaine next week.

Avignon at last

> 'Sur le pont d'Avignon…
> Les beaux messieurs font comme çà
> Les belle dames font comme çà.
> …Et puis encore comme çà.'

We've awarded ourselves high marks for determination. After all, we said we should; we hoped we could …and in the event and just as we'd anticipated, Avignon *Cité des Papes* was well worth all the effort, albeit two years, two cars and two terriers late.

Après the Mistral's recent dire effects the forecast was fair and our midweek timing appropriate - not too much traffic to impede progress - so maps consulted, off we set.

The motorway north successfully navigated,

negotiating the city's hectic industrial conurbations was not too difficult. Thankful for excellent *Centre Ville* route signs, without too much loss of time or temper we soon found ourselves once more before Avignon's medieval ramparts. There to my horror, we realise that the wise city burghers have significantly reduced the parking space hitherto available outside the walls. Another session of dancing round the ring road seems inevitable but, and thank goodness there's always a 'but', matters improved. With but the merest of fits and starts, we quickly discover a massive underground car park dedicated to the *Palais des Papes*, either new or more likely overlooked during our earlier session of waltzing *tous en rond, comme çà*. Waiting at traffic lights ready to cross the ring road and about to enter this miracle of good fortune and city planning, I venture that the city counsellors must have read my book. My wife is unimpressed and on the back seat the dogs by now weary from my epic labours, curl up in Darcey's house for more rest and recuperation.

Dominated by its medieval pontifical stronghold and bordered by similarly impressive papal architecture, and the rather less inspiring entrance to the municipal car park, the palace square is a magnificent public space. Here we quickly discover a popular tourist cafe for a restorative coffee before our much overdue exploration commences.

Avignon's rich history stretches back before the Romans but it was during the early 14th century that the city rose to prominence by becoming a proverbial and desirable port in a storm for the papacy, and thus of interest to historians and tourists ever since.

At this point a word or two of explanation is probably

185

useful. It seems that nowhere is it set in stone that popes are obliged to reside in Rome, consequently during most of the 13th century, due mainly to competing European factionalism for, among other things, control of the Church's vast and powerful secular interests, the papal court tended to wander from place to place. Ostensibly this peripatetic lifestyle was undertaken to lessen the risk to body and soul and I imagine, also designed to protect the papacy's not unsubstantial worldly assets and influence. Thus in the year of Our Lord 1309, faced with increasing hostility from Rome's militant aristocracy, the French pope, Clement V, bestirred himself and brought his court to Avignon. Here it remained throughout the reigns of six French pontiffs until 1377 when Gregory XI upped anchor and returned the Barque of Peter to Rome.

Of course, having the papal court in residence was something of a social and economic cachet bestowing much status, prestige and naturally, increased wealth, on the various towns and cities selected to host it. No doubt much vexed with poor Gregory XI, who conveniently died, the by now mainly French influenced curia, assisted in no small part by the Roman mob's rowdy demands for a city born but if needs must, Italian, pope, in true style - and shades of today's European Commission - simply ignored the legitimate election of the Napolese Urban VI. After holding their own conclave, a rump of French cardinals promptly decamped back to Avignon having elected Robert of Geneva as Pope Clement VII. Thus was contrived what is described as the Great Western Schism, which saw Roman pontiffs competing for leadership of the Church with Avignon's anti-popes and others. This parlous state of affairs lasted until the Council of Constance in 1417, which eventually decided the issue in favour of Rome. As a fascinating aside, an earlier Council of Pisa assembled to resolve matters, quickly declared 'A plague on both your houses' and elected a third pope, Alexander V. Interesting times - the Church Militant seems as good a description as any.

The early medieval *Palais des Papes* is interesting; a well-ordered confusion of bastion, palace and religious centre and, a reflection of the times, probably constructed in much that order. In the intervening years it's been knocked about a bit, particularly during the French revolution; indeed the adjacent Cathedral of Our Lady of the Dome was used as a prison for aristocratic royalists and various anti revolutionary miscreants. Nowadays much care and restoration is being lavished upon this historic site.

Entering the palace through the Champeaux gate by way of an imposing steep flight of steps, equally impressive towers and ramparts soar high above. In keeping with the setting I'm halfway minded to turn and bestow my blessing on the crowds below until firmly restrained by You Know Who.

Access to the Court of Honour is gained through erstwhile guardrooms, now bereft of their martial Defenders of the Faith and these days entirely given over to more worldly pursuits and the collection of fees. Here conveniently but more often not, we tag along behind guided tours of excitable French 6th formers and solemn Japanese tourists as they wend a cat's cradle course around crenellations, courtyards, clerestories, chambers, churches and chapels.

We admire primitive frescoes, some religious, many

not; a rogues' gallery of Avignon's popes; fine architectural models illustrating the Palace's development; echoing naves; a massive banqueting hall; the consistory; conclave apartments; and an obligatory restaurant with its not to be missed *vue panoramique* to tempt the hungry among us.

En route the papal dressing room, bed chamber and study seemed exceptionally well appointed for medieval men of the cloth who, clearly at the top of their game, were surely more interested in God than Mammon - maybe not? With recent examples of similarly imperfect government ministers and parliamentarians firmly in mind, we pass on.

Eventually and by now reeling from a surfeit of papal history, we are guided to depart the palace buildings through the rear tradesmen's entrance - naturally! Before leaving we are deftly manoeuvred into a small but very well stocked wine cellar where, denied the opportunity for a *dégustation*, we do not tarry. Following closely on is the mandatory and much less appealing souvenir shop, which we avoid at a brisk canter before finding ourselves outside blinking in the sunlight of the street.

Undaunted we wend our weary way to the Cathedral of Our Lady of the Dome. This is to be found hard by the papal palace, a stiff climb but well worth the effort. No vast St Peter's, this is a much less pretentious, almost homely basilica but one that still manages to engender no little awe. I was interested to see the papal coronation throne preserved in some splendour but frankly, rather overshadowed by a magnificent, no doubt much later, church organ. Not to be outdone, its gilded pipes glitter richly, touched here and there by shafts of sunlight amid the gloom of the nave. Some of the cathedral's side chapels contain the tombs of Avignon's popes and in one a statue of the bridge building Saint Bénézet, heaving his great block of stone even yet, has a restorative wine flask to hand. This sighting prompts timely motivation so, abandoning piety in favour of sinful ways, we descend to our preferred cafe for a well deserved cold beer.

While finishing our welcome drinks an impromptu brass band strikes up to see us on our way. A dozen or so rather gifted players arrive to perch like crows in a row on the square's stone traffic bollards, there to entertain the throng. The cheerful ensemble's enthusiastic trumpet solos underscored with much booming bass, echo and reverberate around the square where mercifully they drown out their much less professional competition. Today this comprises rather unhappy but excruciatingly hyperactive teenage break-dancers whose frenzied accompaniment emanates from a seriously outgunned ghetto blaster. As befitting their inferior status these morose discontents, perform and frown from their less salubrious and far from prestigious position near the car park's equally dismal entrance. Here until thankfully thwarted, they attempt and patently fail, to wow the crowds before abandoning the attempt and slinking off - stage left. I expect they'll spray paint some graffiti for an encore.

Following a Must Not Be Missed detour through the Place de L'Horlogue with its cafes, carousel and shade trees, all topped off by a wonderful clock with articulated characters to ring the changes high above, we return to the Jeep to find our way home.

What a wonderful day's outing.

It's magic!

Tea and toast for breakfast has become a bit of a tradition when we're away - one that I much enjoy. Strangely it's a pleasure we don't normally indulge in at home. In her day Darcey loved it because she'd always get a nibble of the butt end of my toast, spread with butter and marmalade of course. In typical doggy fashion she came to accept this treat as her due and would sit head cocked, patient and unblinking, watching every mouthful until her turn came. The dog's longing gaze was often so intense that we endowed her with the power to levitate toast, although in truth, she never quite managed that feat. In time *ergo propter hoc*, she became quite fussy, to the extent of declining her delicacy should we have the downright temerity to skimp on the butter. Treat or not, dry toast was just not an option, being neither acceptable nor to be tolerated, and she made sure we knew it.

Surprise, surprise! The Guys have started to display the same characteristics - to the extent that we now realize that Sam doesn't care for dry toast. Elle, naturally, is less discerning.

In a futile attempt to break this undesirable behaviour my wife, who it will be remembered is the officer-in-charge of dog training, has taken to ensuring that Sam's toast has a generous spread of butter before it's offered. Even then it's subjected to careful scrutiny and several sniffs before being graciously and delicately accepted. This morning we were amused by his contortions to retrieve a delicious smear that somehow became deposited, just out of reach on his muzzle. We've no intention of showing them but now think that they'll do well in agility competitions. The Buttered Toast and Marmalade Novice Hurdles sounds about right.

Camargue   *Once more and with feeling*

The Camargue's allure has been drawing us back consequently there's been plotting and planning at Le petit mas de l'Aupière. Last time we concentrated our efforts by way of a northbound arc around the Étang de Vaccarès but on this visit we'd like to swing south to see the lagoons and dunes bordering the Mediterranean Sea. Our handy tourist guide has a pictorial map, which suggests we can drive from Salin de Giraud to Les Saintes Maries de le Mere by way of a narrow causeway taking in the Phare de la Gacholle lighthouse on the way. So far so good and a short while later a second ten minute voyage over the Grand Rhône, no ancient Greek Odyssey but great fun, saw us safely ashore. A circuitous route eventually brings us to the *étang's* eastern edge where we turn south before the going gets tough and the Jeep got going. The four by four Wrangler proves a triumph, coping easily with the potholed gravel laid tracks and byways where a surprising number of rather aggressive sleeping *gendarme*s have been laid to trap the unwary. Quite why this should be is yet another mystery. It's not as if anyone would ever imagine the binocular bedecked bird watchers of the world as ton-up kids requiring such hostile deterrence. It's difficult to imagine droves of Volkswagen camper vans burning rubber in the Camargue, but no doubt *Nounou* Knows Best. If asked, I intend to recommend Gatso speed trap cameras as suitable substitutes for the Twitchers' tripod mounted, long lens Kodaks, Nikons and Cannons.

191

Allowing for the heavy going and using all the Jeep's remarkable cross country capacity, a sedate but bumpy ride eventually deposits us at a tiny lay-by far short of the lighthouse. Here our proposed route is barred by unforeseen impregnable barriers and a multiplicity of no entry signs. It seems that not even the Guys may pass this point and so, unmoved in the face of beastly bureaucracy, they continue to take life easy, relaxing in Darcey's house. Try as we might, further motorized progress towards distant Les Saintes Maries de le Mere is to be denied us. *Monsieur*, lightly engaged in essential maintenance of an antique sluice gate and clearly an expert on local affairs, is consulted.

'Non! Absolument pas!' Four wheel drive or not, low ratio or not, tricolour aflutter or not, it's to be the northbound route for *l'anglais* once more - and that's it and all about it!

Disappointed but not downhearted and with much careful shunting to negotiate a very narrow much rutted earthen embankment, we reverse course.

We're content to have seen flocks of flamingos clucking and chuckling together while tiptoeing their ridiculous way in the brine. Among the pools and shallows they compete with brilliantly white egrets, herons, hawks and many more common species of waterfowl. After my disappointment in Normandy and not to be outdone, I catch a glimpse of a solitary otter; bronzed and stately as it sleekly navigates its preferred watercourse in search of lunch. You Know Who, from her place in the cheap seats on the right hand drive Jeep's temporary offside, is thus denied the opportunity and is glum. Clearly the requirement to drive on the right in

France is my fault and some cunning plan solely designed to interfere with her view of the local fauna.

Later we motor over to the Petite Camargue, which lies to the west of the Petite Rhône, to inspect Aigues Mortes' fine bastions, and what a sight awaits us there. This long redundant, now landlocked Mediterranean seaport witnessed the departure of two 13th century crusading armies to carry out their divinely inspired but no doubt secularly subsidised, mission against errant infidels. Later during the turbulent 15th and 16th centuries Aigues Mortes was legitimised as a sanctuary for dissenting Protestants but in the next, many Huguenots, dismissing the invitation to convert to Catholicism, were imprisoned within its walls. Poor culpable God; it would seem he has a lot to answer for.

Whilst on the fascinating subject of sin and temptation, in Hemingway's novel *The Garden of Eden* he sets his characters' honeymoon scenes in romantic Aigues Mortes, where in a classic *ménage à trois* they both fall in love with Marita.

The town's crenellated battlements, tall towers and robust gates, all built in attractively weathered pale stone, enclose a regular layout of streets and buildings that shape its antique heart. Compared with Avignon's similarly appealing but much less sturdy ramparts, they are a persuasive study in the art of medieval defence and, to this amateur historian, just as attractive.

Having successfully resisted both the Black Death and the predations of time, Aigues Mortes is even yet, resolutely complete, more or less undamaged and mercifully free of pestilent graffiti.

In equal measure awestruck and captivated, we fully expect a pageant of mounted *chevaliers*, 'Their banners bravely spread', to ride forth; emerging out of the mists of time from beneath the raised portcullis of a narrow gateway some time soon.

This is an enchanted place apparently dropped unspoiled and unscathed into the 21st century from a legendary and chivalric past. Isolated, secure and breathtakingly splendid, yet for all that rather nonchalant, it stands poised, ready to welcome Hollywood's cast of camera crews and directors but clearly offers little for set designers.

In comparison with the Camargue's extensive wetlands we found the Petite Camargue to be a much more fertile, somewhat softer environment, with many vineyards and much agriculture waiting to be discovered. We'd like to see more, lots more, but time and tide wait for no man and regretful that our earlier unplanned detour has eaten away our day, we leave the unsullied romantic glamour of Aigues Mortes and turn for home

…but, as I've observed before, therein lies opportunity.

🐕 🐕

We passed a Wrangler in the Camargue and just yesterday another in Istres, this time an exact double of ours, albeit soft topped. No doubt you can guess the rest.

Au revoir Provence

It's almost Easter and we're getting ready to move on. Since we're due to arrive in Aquitaine late on Good Friday eve we anticipate a little difficulty with restocking there so You Know Who has made a little list of necessities. Standing before our preferred supermarket's stack of microwave meals inspecting the runners and riders, my wife was audibly astonished to discover a dish of pork and bananas. When we lived abroad, particularly in Malaysia, we ate some pretty odd things but pork with bananas - surely not? Closer inspection is clearly required and with the timely assistance of my reading spectacles, shortly all is revealed: *'Porc, sauce Aigre Douce, Riz et Morceaux d'Ananas'* is not quite what she took it to be.

'Non, mon petite legume, not Bananas - *d'Ananas!* It's Chinese Sweet and Sour Pork with Rice and - Pineapple chunks!'

We collapse in gales of mirth. Nearby French shoppers are bemused.

🐕 🐕

We've only one more day here before we depart for Aquitaine and this evening, long after night has fallen, I take the Guys for a late stroll in the tranquil darkened garden. After a turbulent rain swept day, an almost full Eastertide moon rides high in the clear sky, softly illuminating the *étang's* but recently becalmed waters. Framed by the now familiar darkly silhouetted pines and olives, the distant lights of the far shore sparkle and twinkle like a jewelled necklace while above, cryptic star signs glitter in the silence of eternity. Spellbound we pause, the dogs alert but motionless, while I attempt to consider a suitable literary conclusion for our month at Le petit mas de l'Aupière. For the moment defeated we return indoors where a well-deserved treat awaits my faithful friends.

Provence, it seems, has a lyrical effect on me.

Chapter Seven

Plaisance Dordogne

Dithyramb

Good Friday is all but done. In the hearth the logs
have burned down to a warm bed of glowing embers and,
after a hectic couple of days, You Know Who is already
fast asleep upstairs. Following her lead the Guys are
curled up nose to tail near the fire, where they are
energetically engaged in doggie dreams of today's
excitements exploring the new estate. Outside in the
dark of night, the modest din of *provençal* cicadas has been
replaced by mere cacophony. A determined but invisible
band of *Pays de Bastides* bullfrogs are performing at full
throttle. Their raucous serenade comes accompanied by
sporadic counterparts - descants from a chorus of not to
be outdone, resident ducks. The resulting uproar makes
for a far from melodious lullaby so, taking full advantage
of this somewhat less than tranquil opportunity, I settle
down to work. With the aid of a glass or two of *vin rouge* I
almost succeed in organising a few thoughts.

Time and tide

Before leaving Istres last week we were curious when
our hostess suddenly varied her hitherto rigid routine,
suddenly coming and going at different times. All is now
clear. Without bothering to tell us, some objectionable
French bureaucrat has changed the clocks. With
thoroughly bad grace I'd already accommodated an
hour's difference during our Channel crossing and a

fortnight ago, courtesy of the Internet, we'd accidentally caught up with the start of British Summer Time - requiring yet more complicated adjustments. Now it seems we've failed to appreciate that France also employs seasonal time variations. In keeping with the spirit of horrid EU integration, these events can't possibly be permitted to take place in collaboration with the UK's changes - *naturellement!* Thus, blissfully ignorant, we registered France's march of time a week late and then only courtesy of the *autoroute's* electronic caution signs, which conveniently become a clock when not otherwise engaged. This, less than pleasing, discovery was the only significant or remotely interesting interlude in a rather tedious cross-country drive to Aquitaine. I hate governments' intrusive fondness for faffing about with time. 'Spring forward - Fall back' and the rest of the unmitigated nonsense associated with completely unnecessary alterations to my body clock and the Guys' routine, is a bore. In the absence of intelligible destructions, the Jeep's radio clock is now two hours adrift and likely to remain so.

Livery and maintenance

Domaine de la Villote lies in rolling countryside not too far south of Bergerac and is typical of the old-established, rather imposing farmsteads that are commonly to be found hereabouts. A one time stables and stud farm serving a nearby *château*, its grandeur is now faded and much of its living long lost to the ravages of time and the vagaries of economics. The estate is now owned by an English couple who, inheriting it in derelict condition, care enough to restore it to its former glory.

The ongoing refurbishment, another Herculean labour of love, clearly involves prodigious effort, outrageous investment and I suspect, occasional heartache, but this is all well concealed within displays of insufferable energy and slightly smug satisfaction. Having converted one or two of the buildings and with much still to do, they augment the work-in-progress with holiday cottage rentals and a bed and breakfast business. I envy their entrepreneurial enterprise and enthusiastic renovation. We hope they'll succeed in their, as yet somewhat tenuous, venture. The *Maison de maître* will be a joy when eventually fully restored.

We enter the property by way of a chalky, rather waterlogged narrow causeway which crosses a stylish but not quite Roman, stone bridge separating attractive deciduous copses that are just budding into leaf. Pretty babbling brooks, their banks populated by boisterous variegated ducks and seriously outnumbered geese, flow beneath to replenish a small, island bedecked, trout lake. Elsewhere there are paddocks with horses and ponies and around the yards, outbuildings and barns a harem of dutiful chickens pays court to a magnificent cock. This splendid chap, caparisoned in glossy shades of light and dark bronze, is blessed with tail plumes of glorious dark turquoise, a bright red comb and a shrewd and discerning eye. Standing head and shoulders above the roost, he struts and stalks to beguile and delight his adoring concubines, while harrying his lacklustre adolescent competitors into abject submission.

The damp lane shortly snakes to the rear of a weathered, clunch built *maison principale*. This is a broad two-storey affair with a low-pitched roof of elderly slates topped off by a brace of prominent chimneys. Its rendered external façade is uniformly pierced by oriels and elegantly tall windows, their old-fashioned square panes and faded blue shutters lending charisma and character to the property. Befitting the nature of its equine heritage, the chief elevation of the building overlooks its former stable yard at the rear. Entry is gained by way of a broad gateway that pierces an adjacent stable block which is crowned by a charming, albeit rather crooked, pigeon loft. Framed within, balustraded double stairways of worn stone are to be seen. Rising to a small terrace that commands the space beneath, they lead indoors between further stylish windows and shutters. The timber braced stables and a detached coach house, boasting yet another but much less lop-sided *pigeonnier*, form an open square - now transformed into a slightly less than formal garden of striking proportions.

I later discover that some of the main building's underlying masonry is possibly Roman though our host confesses that he has been unable to identify the particular stonework in question.

In the course of conversation it transpires that we share similar martial antecedents so, being kindred spirits to the extent of swapping unlikely war stories, I am disinclined to disbelieve him.

Weekend de Pâques

Like Provence's recent Mistral it seems that bad weather is determined to plague our visit. According to our hostess, last week's conditions were a joy but there has been torrential rain ever since and in a Bergerac *tabac*, while I cling to an uncertain parking space without, and my wife reluctantly satisfies my cigar fix within, *Madame* is forecasting more of the same until next week.

Undaunted by some fairly sharp downpours we take the time to drive south in order to carry out a reconnaissance. Tomorrow is Easter Sunday and an Anglican Communion service has been organised which my wife is keen to attend. Since the padre, a peripatetic soul whose parish allegedly encompasses Malta as well as Aquitaine is leading the effort as well as the rites, it seems churlish to deny him his congregation and You Know Who's wishes to contribute to it.

With but little of the usual map reading confusion and trifling differences of opinion, we scout the proposed outbound route using a by now obligatory *interesting* detour and eventually locate the church. On our way back we take the opportunity for a fleeting stop in Eymet, our previous base when we last visited this area. It being mid afternoon on a Saturday, Eymet, in shades of dismal Langres, was shut. Denied coffee or a more sensible and by this time much needed, restorative we return to the cottage to walk the Guys and indulge in some energetic relaxation in front of the fire. In redemption for my sinful ways and heretical opinions I shall surely be summoned at some ungodly hour to take You Know Who to church. I doubt I shall be granted an Indulgence for my efforts.

'Have a nice pray'

Easter morning ...and Monteton has been occupied by the British. In our turn we arrive at this small hamlet

201

situated high above Le Dropt's wide river valley via a narrow winding road lined by regimented orchards of fruit trees. Appropriately and despite intermittent lashing spring showers, they are just coming into glorious fresh seasonal blossom.

In the village a miniature church square is packed to bursting with cars and our Jeep, while expatriate Church of England worshippers, reinforced by a scattering of hardy tourists, assemble to celebrate Easter.

On loan for the duration, Monteton's *église* is an antique study in old cold stone and youthful stained glass which glows warmly from within tiny arched windows set high above. Underfoot, despite the presence of largely inadequate patio heaters, freezing floor tiles provide ample opportunity for penance while overhead the austere vaulted nave is dominated by a chillingly realistic crucifixion.

Within these Spartan surroundings, very British, Barbour jacketed and Marks & Sparks outfitted parishioners make properly pious entrances, worship and, their devotions done, depart via a clearly popular but excruciatingly well-mannered Meet and Greet with the assembled clergy. Religious duty done, a gentle constitutional within the precincts comes with hot coffee and biscuits as a secular substitute for sacramental bread and wine and banal chatter replaces the liturgy.

Now sustained in both body and soul, we make our way to the Jeep and observe that some enterprising soul had taken the opportunity to provide an English language paperback book exchange. Unattended in the forecourt, the rather dog eared collection of novels, biographys and travel guides lays forlorn and unloved awaiting passing interest from the largely disinterested throng. From their appearance and condition we assume that they (*the books and the congregation!*) are all *fatigué* from their arduous *bonne vie en France?*

Being a long lapsed member of the Bells and Smells Brigade and musically dyslexic I'm clearly no authority, but on reflection the choir and music seemed quite good. I especially enjoyed the combination of traditional Easter anthems and thoroughly British hymns ancient and modern. The old reliables were accompanied by some locally influenced musical interludes conducted by a diminutive but very energetic lady who, in her determination for absolute perfection, took no prisoners. The sermon was interminable, as all sermons should be, and throughout the whole protracted business various fervent functionaries bustled about busily - clearly doing not much at all. Apart from the occasionally toe-tapping music, it all seemed comfortably familiar, much the same as my wife's congregation at home. Thankfully, You Know Who enjoyed her devotions - and the church.

In the car park, a prison break has been staged. Elle, clearly bored by Easter duties, has forced her way out of Darcey's house and made herself just a tad more comfortable on both of the Jeep's front seats. Sam, in an opportunistic takeover bid, remains snug within and is spread out fast asleep. Order is quickly restored and Elle, displaying much bad grace, is re-incarcerated. After much effort removing a surfeit of dog hair further progress may be made. The Jeep's interior fascias have always needed a little care and attention as their rigid plastic is rather vulnerable. Quite what we'll do about the paw marks on the dashboard is a problem for another day. This says much about my more relaxed attitude regarding the care of cars, their parking and my dogs. Had this been the Saab it would have been parked a damp country mile away so as to avoid careless D&Ds, and my outrage at Elle's conduct would surely have been heard across the valley. With the tough Jeep - *C'est la vie!*

Back at Issigeac, as yet unpardoned for my heretical misdemeanours and not quite covered in glory for my heroic churchgoing efforts, I had earmarked but not reserved a table at a likely looking restaurant for a post devotional Sunday lunch. Arriving hotfoot from *piété de Pâques* I was depressed to find it full and thus closed to the tardy. A rapid and slightly desperate reconnaissance quickly revealed an acceptable alternative nearby and this windfall was speedily exploited before we could be repulsed again. In the event our replacement venue proved an excellent substitute. Served by attentive young waitresses we dined in understated style alongside a quietly animated party celebrating a birthday. *Grandpère* with his fifteen or so family and friends had a great time which, from ringside, we enjoyed quite as much as they.

Our *entrée* was chosen from a lavish and beautifully presented self-service cold buffet of wonderful variety. This delight was followed by a delicious *rosé* roast of garlic infused lamb served with lightly *sautéed* spring vegetables all accompanied by a rather decent local Bordeaux. After a brisk turn through a wealth of excellent cheeses I simply could not eat more and so, declining a gentle ramble through the selection of sumptuous desserts, settled for espresso. Someone, who may not be named, managed pudding and cream laden cappuccino!

After wishing Granddad happy birthday and bidding *Au revoir* to the guests and *les jolies serveuses* who looked after us, we depart for the cottage and well-deserved *après midi* snoozing with the dogs.

Stargazing

Last night we took the Guys out for a late constitutional and were simply bewitched by the night sky. Cloud cover was sparse and in the clear countryside air, the stars appeared more intense that ever we see them from our usual Pennine slopes. Bright bejewelled constellations of sparkling diamonds formed a veritable pageant in the night sky as Springtide's zodiac passed in review - and among the glitz and glitter gentle Venus exhibited her more virtuous golden hue. Quite a show, and apart from the vociferous bullfrogs, one completely lacking the customary racket from our home motorway, or the rather intrusive commentaries usually to be endured in a planetarium. All in all a much better performance and entirely free.

L'anglais abroad

Eymet's Thursday morning market received our undivided attention today. We always enjoy the hustle and bustle of French markets particularly when they are to be found in the *Pays de Bastides* where the medieval townships' central squares were designed and built with just such activities in mind. As ever it gave us the opportunity to browse and indulge ourselves among the fruit and veg and various other unmissable delights. A welcome espresso and cigar in the cool of one of the open arcades that invariably surround the marketplaces completed the treat. Later we dropped in to say hello to the owners of the B&B where we stayed previously, only to discover they were on the cusp of leaving for a few days in England. We've agreed to pop back for a longer chin-wag before leaving for Normandy next week.

🐕 🐕

I'm always amused by Eymet - a little piece of England *en* France. Actually is not the town that makes me laugh so much as the curious expansiveness of the expatriate British who form a significant and unavoidable rump of its population. English as well as French, is regularly heard in the shops, cafes and its market. To a man and woman the expats seem to lose their innate British reserve and adopt a larger than life, rather 'hail fellow well met' attitude when out and about - something I'm fairly sure they wouldn't dream of doing in the UK. Today *Monsieur* was clearing a table at the cafe and dropped some cutlery. The anticipated: *'Merde!'* was replaced by an unexpected: 'Bugger!' which I think amply demonstrates my point.

We've been restocking at a large supermarket in the outskirts of Bergerac. Whilst engaged among the grub and booze and just to reinforce my earlier opinions, marketing announcements are made in French and English!

Happy snaps

In order to satisfy her photographic lusts but denied the opportunity on Sunday when the weather was atrocious, my wife has demanded a return visit to

Monteton to capture its church for posterity. The fruit trees are now in full bloom and seen from afar the *église* seems to float in drifts of white blossom.

Although a bit of a haul I'm glad we came however, in order to preserve my carefully nurtured but largely bogus, irreligious and inartistic standing, I am not minded to reveal this to You Know Who for fear of further sneering.

Bastides

I love the ambience of the *Bastides*. Within the remains of their battlemented walls, crooked, timber framed, medieval houses jostle cheek by jowl in narrow streets around their arcaded formal market squares and grand churches.

In the mid 12th century the lovely heiress Eleanor of Aquitaine, divorced former Queen of Louis VII of France, married the 19 year-old Duke of Normandy and Count of Anjou, Henry Plantagenet - later Henry II of England and eleven years her junior. This marriage - some argue a love match, others, a clever ploy by Henry to acquire Eleanor's vast inheritance and influence - led to political turbulence and open warfare for control of the western coastal lands and territories which stretched from Flanders to the Pyrenees. It was in this fraught state of affairs that by royal decree, the fortified *Bastides* were originally established, some being built by the English others by the French.

Generally dominating hilltops and designed for defence, their infrastructure was more often planned in a lattice of streets and lanes and each retains a unique character and charm. Within its walls towers and gates,

English commissioned Monpazier is formally laid out in an unbroken grid pattern with a huge marketplace forming its heart. Eymet and Villeréal are neither fish nor fowl; sometimes following the prescribed chequerboard pattern but often muddled according to geography, their manner of construction and further growth - but each have central markets and churches. On the other hand, narrow Beaumont with its magnificent church is a defended strip village sited to control the road south east from Bergerac to Monpazier.

Competing for attention, charming medieval Issigeac, not quite a Bastide, is a rather rambling affair; originally a walled settlement and religious stronghold with a prominent bishop's palace at its heart. Due to its uncertain heritage and therefore lacking a dedicated formal open marketplace, the popular Sunday trading arrangements are something of an afterthought, taking place along the lanes and byways throughout the settlement.

After today's weekly market there was to be a *Concours de Soupe*, a grand affair, which promised much interesting overindulgence throughout the remnants of a pleasant sunny afternoon. We were strongly minded to give Issigeac's hotly competitive soup kitchen some serious and considered attention but in the event another milestone lunch spoiled our appetites and thus interfered with our plans.

We've enjoyed and lingered over another Sunday spectacular at our preferred Issigeac restaurant …and having stumbled on a delicious local *vin blanc brut* to accompany our scrumptious seared chicken, we return home disgracefully full to discover the afternoon is all but gone. Fulfilling an earlier promise, our hosts kindly gave us an equally grand and much appreciated, tour of their *maison* to make up for missing the soup tournament. Much like prospective buyers we poke and prod and 'Ooh' and 'Ah' around the house while our animated guides radiate enthusiastic architectural highs interspersed with tight-lipped lows when they consider the labour and no doubt reflect on the costs.

Betwixt and between the inevitable clutter of a temporary abode and sporadic building site, their legacy is a rather sad prospect nowadays. There are, however, many wonderful early features crying out for the care and attention which is gradually being lavished on them. Above, amid wretchedly peeling ceilings, there are still crisp, plasterwork roundels and unspoiled, rather stylish, cornices to be seen - and admired. Dominated by an imposing fireplace, the principal sitting room has tactile carved and moulded fitted pine cabinets, their serpentine auburn curves completely filling one wall, where they surround an elegant doorway. In places there are early, possibly original, silk wall coverings - now woefully neglected, dejected and defunct and unlikely to be retained.

Despite some of its *enfilade* design weaknesses I was pleased to learn that our hosts' intend to retain most of the building's slightly awkward earlier layout. This decision clearly flies in the face of many of today's tastes for convenience and privacy and no doubt it was a difficult choice but one that I applaud. Also against the trend, they have decided to resist many modern restoration techniques and temptations. Undoubtedly these would ensure a speedy and probably cheaper, completion of the project but surely at the cost of its period features. On balance I think they're absolutely right to retain the building's essential atmosphere and character.

卅 卅

Just recently we've been accompanied on our morning walks by one of our hosts' dogs; a hairy character who barges ahead in an appropriately proprietorial manner. We trek around the estate's ploughed fields and half way into our walk the Lad put up a magnificent hare. Frankly he didn't have the legs for prolonged pursuit and quickly gave up the chase. Thankfully the Guys failed to spot the opportunity; only getting excited when they picked up the scent long after the quarry had fled the scene. The Lad, a much older dog and much taken with the attention and the treats, has been a bit of a calming influence on the Guys. This is something that we might exploit when we return home - now only nine days hence.

On our way back to the cottage with some semblance of order restored, our hostess, heavily engaged in gardening, points out a baby red squirrel clinging to a nearby tree trunk. It's the first time for ages that I've had the opportunity to see a red squirrel as our home population are exclusively grey but I have vague recollections of occasional sightings in my New Forest boyhood. Later I discovered that the squirrel had been abandoned and our hosts decided to attempt to hand rear it. They were looking a little ragged from the early morning feeding regime before we left but I understand that the squirrel was making the best of a bad lot. After we'd returned home we continued to get occasional reports strongly reminiscent of puppy rearing. I suspect

Monsieur Écureuil rouge will do all right for himself.

A good egg

Hector the cockerel is clearly giving his full measure of devotion, as a result we've been feasting on the estate's fresh eggs and what a joy they are. Far removed from our regular supermarket's rather pallid offerings, these home grown delicacies come with bespeckled fawn shells accommodating copious subtle whites which, in their turn, enfold generous rich yolks of a deep golden hue. You Know Who made delightfully light omelettes but frankly I preferred them lightly boiled when - attended by ranks of buttered toast soldiers ready to be dipped deep into their luscious interiors - they were mouth wateringly delicious. On those rare occasions when there's only one egg for breakfast one would do well to remember; '…that at Domaine de la Villote one egg is an *oeuf!*' Well-done Hector …and the girls.

Adieu Aquitaine

Yet again today's weather has been glorious but our time has been occupied with administration and packing as we move on to Normandy tomorrow. We shall miss the historic *Pays de Bastides* and the stylish but as yet unfinished, Domaine de la Villote with its thoughtful hosts, substantial dog-friendly estate, generous menagerie and vociferous bullfrogs. We've managed to revisit many favourite *Bastides* and narrowly avoided traipsing around the area's many *châteaux* - as well as Bordeaux …but, and as has been said before, therein lies opportunity.

Chapter Eight

Gueures Haute-Normandie

Our pause in Normandy was always intended as a breather, a time for reflection, administration and maintenance before heading home.

Delightful Gueures is a small rural escape not far from Dieppe and we'd thought that it might make a useful base to explore Bayeux and Normandy's Overlord battlefields. In the event, especially as our itinerary proved unrealistic, we took advantage of our stay to draw breath and see to the Guys' pet passport treatments before heading to Calais and home.

Thank goodness we had *Post hoc* built flexibility into our cunning travel plans because a malevolent Icelandic volcano disrupted air travel, which in turn badly affected Channel ferries. Denied the Internet and only after much fraught mobile telephony we eventually secured passage with dependable P&O only a day or so earlier than we'd originally intended.

This was our first visit to Dieppe, which we found uncannily similar to North Yorkshire's Whitby; even to the extent of having an abbey church situated high on cliffs opposite from where it overlooks the harbour. Both small ports are slightly frenetic, slightly scruffy and slightly down-market holiday destinations and only tolerable in good weather.

Originally based about fishing and cross channel commerce, nowadays Dieppe thrives on seaside vacation trade and maintains its ferry service although to a much lesser degree than Calais.

After careful consideration and parading just a little patriotic prejudice, we've decided that Whitby has it by a short head.

A couple of days later after the usual outrage and uproar at the vets, the officer-in-charge, the dogs, the Jeep and I found ourselves safely settled in P&O's comfortable aquatic embrace and heading for home.

It's been a fine couple of months that we all thoroughly enjoyed. Whilst weary from travel and pleased to be home we're already deep in plans for our next adventure. The dogs have not been consulted.

Chapter Nine

Pensée après-coup

The Guys

My friend is frequently to be found dog-sitting Oscar, his daughter's Husky Alsatian cross. This is something he much enjoys and consequently encourages but rarely admits. Just recently over a glass or two, we fell to mulling; comparing progress, training and inevitably, the Guys' behaviour on holiday abroad. Naturally, but in the face of recent evidence to the contrary, I defended their manners. Truth be told they are improving, albeit more slowly than I'd like - especially when visitors call and Elle falls victim to uncontrolled excitement. My friend reflected that, whilst they are undoubtedly calming down, in comparison with our adolescent hooligans, Darcey was a real lady and he compared her to comfortable slippers. I was hard pressed to disagree. We miss her yet and she'll always have a special place in our hearts.

All in all the Guys really were not too much of a trial but I'm not sure that, if asked, Domaine de la Villote's chickens and ducks would necessarily agree with my opinion. Yes, touring with them has its limitations. Yes, the Pet Passport requirements are awkward and expensive. Yes, not every cottage takes dogs ...but on balance the sheer pleasure of their company far outweighed the encumbrances. We are, it has to be admitted, inveterate doggy folk and just to prove the point enquiries are well in hand for a return to the Loire for a month in the late summer.

Regrets for things not done

Unfortunately our friends did not manage their long weekend at Eymet; no doubt we'll manage better next time.

Nimes, the spiritual home of denim, as well as Bayeux and Caen cleverly managed to avoid our scrutiny. Frankly we're not too bothered about the former but now think a longer visit to Normandy is required. Whilst we love the Lubéron especially Bonnieux, we've still not bothered to seek out Peter Mayle's house near Ménerbes. I doubt we ever will. It was a shame that we missed Carlos Núñez's concert but I expect we'll survive. Our consolation supper was superb.

Our first experience of the Camargue was simply stunning. It had not occurred to us that we could have spent the whole month exploring and photographing its wildlife and scenery. We are determined to return and also to spend more time west of the Petite Rhône. We are currently seeking out accommodation in or near Aigues Mortes for next Spring.

...and things that linger

Weeks after we returned home muddy evidence of Domaine de la Villote's sodden chalk track continued to emerge from beneath the Jeep to begrime the running boards. Our friends' daughter, who earns much needed knickers money with hose and sponge lavishing attention on the Wrangler, is becoming fractious. To her further chagrin and despite much effort and lashings of polish, the dashboard still bears the scars of Elle's Monteton rampage.

Just the other day whilst dropping our friends at the airport, I enjoyed the last couple of delicious sweets from a packet of French Wether's Originals that sustained our marathon cross-country treks. My wife observed that, given Wether's marketing strategy and my age and condition, they were entirely appropriate refreshments.

Some explanations

In *No Criticisms* I used a couple of chapter sub headings that took my fancy and seemed appropriate at the time. I now confess that the latter caption needed a moment or two's thought before I decided to use it. For those who've managed to stay the course and currently find themselves without a dictionary or the Internet, I offer explanations:

Faugh a Ballagh! In Chapter Six '*Faugh a Ballagh!*' is Gaelic for 'Clear the way!' and is the motto of the Royal Irish Regiment, in my day the Royal Irish Rangers, when I had the pleasure of serving alongside their feisty 2nd Battalion in Berlin. If you've not already done so I strongly recommend hearing the Regiment's Pipes and Drums playing the lively quick march of the same name.

Dithyramb. To be found in Chapter Seven, *Dithyramb*, which earns a decent Scrabble score, was a frenzied ancient Greek chorus with booze and dancing held in honour of Dionysus, the god of wine and orgies. What with my hysterical Bullfrog choir, several alcoholic nightcaps and much literary desperation, it seemed appropriate. I avoided late night terpsichorean carousing - You Know Who might have objected.

One or two other quotes deserve a mention:

'It's just a jump to the left.' Richard O'Brien's excellent 'transvestite, transsexual' and corset clad science fiction musical '*The Rocky Horror Picture Show*', an enduring favourite at Orchard House, is the source of my wife's tune '*Let's do the Time Warp again.*'

'The Church Militant.' The Catholic or

Universal, Church is traditionally divided into: The Church Militant - Christians who are living. The Church Triumphant - Those in Heaven. The Church Penitent - Christians in Purgatory.

'With Banners Bravely Spread.' This is the title of a, not quite Pre Raphaelite, romantic painting by Sir John Gilbert (*1817-1897*) depicting mounted knights riding forth to battle.

'By Air.' The late great and still sadly missed, Michael Flanders, another firm Orchard House favourite, wrote and performed his monologue '*By Air*' for the humorous review '*At the Drop of Another Hat.*' (*Flanders and Swann. 1966.*) I'm still desperate to include a line from their outrageously satirical song '*All Gaul*' somewhere in this manuscript.

Postscript

The end of an era

After her Monteton escape bid, Elle managed another on the voyage home. Fortunately, apart from the usual excess of unwanted dog hair, there was little damage done. On the other hand Darcey's house was looking increasingly fragile and once we returned home it became clear that a replacement was long overdue.

With much regret *chez* Darcey has been consigned to the rubbish tip.

Book Three
The Waif's Tail

Patch

As advertised by Dogs Trust Darlington

Waif (*n.*) (*Orig - 13c., Old French* Guaif)

A person or animal abandoned and forsaken due to adversity, loss or some other circumstances.

Synonyms: Ownerless, unclaimed, flotsam, outcast, orphan, stray animal.

Tail (*n.*)

1. A body of employees or servants who accompany and attend.

Synonyms: Cortège, entourage, following, posse, retinue, suite, train.

2. The part of the body upon which someone sits

Synonyms: Backside, behind, bottom, breech, bum, butt.

3. The sticky out bit that wags.

Chapter One

Adieu

No Criticisms, the second volume of *The Best Deal,* was written in the year 2010; thereafter, whilst we continued to holiday in France and England, I did not feel minded to add to the book believing that it must surely become repetitious and dull. We revisited Northumberland, the West Country, Normandy, the Loire, and Provence and all were relished and recorded but even with new adventures aplenty and our computers' memories stuffed full of photographs, those treasured destinations and our latest experiences of them remained unchronicled.

There matters lay until some twelve years later. Between times Mother Nature took her inevitable course and we all waxed but mostly waned; growing a little older, a little less mobile, and latterly much less disposed to embark on long drives abroad. Oh! The inevitable march of time.

Ever adolescent, the dogs seemed immune to most of these trials and tribulations until early Spring 2022 when Sam, ever a snorer, was beset by serious breathing difficulties. Our vet recommended an X-ray examination and that required Sam to endure a general anaesthetic. Once asleep it was quickly discovered that his heart and lungs were fatally compromised. While painful and heartbreaking the decision to let him go was both obvious and unavoidable. Oh! The obligations and penalties of responsible dog ownership.

We took comfort in the fact that Elle still enjoyed good

health and, although clearly missing her long term partner in crime, she seemed destined to remain firmly in charge at Orchard House for some years yet. It was not to be. In early July she suddenly became distressed and was clearly in much discomfort. A recommended X-ray scan and blood tests performed under general anaesthetic proved inconclusive but later that day, while convalescing at our vet's surgery, she rapidly declined. Faced with the inevitable we agreed that there was no alternative but to let her join dear old Sam.

...and the consensus? 'No more dogs.' Seem familiar? Of course it does. This time we lasted a little less than two months. We are, it has to be admitted, inveterate doggy folk.

Chapter Two

Likely candidates

At this point in our story I would like it to be carefully noted that after Elle's sad end my wife did not dispose of the various canine paraphernalia and artefacts that remained about the house as had happened after we lost dear old Darcey. Instead everything was carefully stowed in the garage. I therefore find it astonishing that, in the matter of welcoming another dog to Orchard House, I am the one alleged to have crumbled first.

With thoroughly bad grace we had accepted that, due to age and ebbing mobility, acquiring a puppy was a non-starter so an alternative Cunning Plan was required. Coincidentally we'd become much concerned about the welfare of abandoned dogs, especially in recent times when the Covid pandemic seems to have dramatically increased the problem.

Not unsurprisingly we're long standing supporters and members of Dogs Trust so, for this irredeemable Parson Russell Terrier devotee, their re-homing Website was a natural port of call. On first inspection the rogues' gallery of deserving homeless dogs was disturbingly large but, as luck would have it, searchable by location, breed and size ...and yes! Parsons figured among the breeds listed there. I was immediately attracted to a middle aged hopeful with soulful eyes who was a chance guest of the Dogs Trust's Evesham re-homing centre. Once again, it should be carefully noted that my wife did not demur when I suggested we start the on-line adoption process: 'Just to see how it works.' Observe as well that I'm hardly inexperienced when it comes to composing a neat turn of phrase so, remarkably for someone determined not to weaken, my wife suddenly found it absolutely essential to help to draft our submission to adopt the dog.

What we both hadn't *quite* appreciated was that experienced Dogs Trust decision makers appraise, sift and classify re-homing applications entirely according to how well they fit the relevant dog's needs. Thereafter, once closely matched hopefuls are identified, they are offered the opportunity to adopt a dog on a first come, first served basis. A few days later a nice e-mail broke the bad news.

Undaunted and with lessons firmly learned, henceforth, and on an almost daily basis, I kept a very close eye on the Trust's runners and riders - tightly supervised by You Know Who.

Late August

Darlington's a bit of a drag from Orchard House but that's where Patch, an elderly Parson who needed just a little care and attention in the evening of his years, was to be found. He'd popped up with a 'New arrival' banner on his photograph and we quickly agreed that he could be the one. With all the benefits accruing from our first rehearsal I submitted our application and then sat back to wait; fully prepared to be disappointed yet again.

But no! The very next afternoon we were telephoned to be interrogated about our submission and informed about Patch's antecedents and health. It turned out that he'd enjoyed a settled family life for his first ten or so years but then, unfortunately and as all too often, his circumstances changed for the worse. The Darlington centre had taken him in and in the short term, he'd been happily fostered. Sometime later after due process he'd been adopted. That arrangement had lasted for just shy of a week until he'd unwisely growled and snapped at his new owners when they tried to turf him off a settee. So, rather than finding his Forever Home, back to the warm embrace of Dogs Trust Darlington he went - not entirely covered in glory!

Dogs Trust: 'Could we cope with this behaviour?'

Me: 'Does the Sun rise in the East?'

Dogs Trust: 'Also Mr Long he's had some lameness in his hind offside leg and is having treatment. Would that be a problem?'

Me: 'We're falling apart at the seams m'dear - he'll be in good company.'

Finally, and before hateful officialdom took over: 'Would we confirm that we'd be prepared to give him a chance?'

With absolutely no hesitation: 'No problems!'

For all that I loathe and therefore try to avoid bureaucracy in all its many guises, under the circumstances I gladly made an exception for Patch, especially because Dogs Trust made adopting him as easy as their policy of protecting the dogs in their care permitted. Given the distance to Darlington I negotiated a dispensation from their usual requirement to undertake at least a couple of Meet and Greet appointments before adopting him. Thus everything was done on the phone and Internet until, after only one or two false starts - mostly down to ensuring Patch's continuing welfare as well as some light contractual protection for us - we were invited to come to the centre and provided all went well, to bring him home.

Chapter Three

Dulce Domum

The Dogs Trust's Darlington re-homing centre is a fine example of charitable funds being put to good use. Situated out of town it occupies an easily found and thankfully, not too remote, retired farmstead. Its bespoke facilities are bright, modern, well appointed and clearly well managed. The retained and volunteer workforce comprise an enthusiastic, caring and very professional team whose dedication to and love for, their hapless charges shines forth. Within the centre's welcoming environment the Trust's administration was obviously well prepared and after only a short delay, due to Patch being already engaged in a prearranged training session - 'No change in routine here!' - we were introduced.

...and that, as they say, was that. Arguably our meeting might be described as preordained. Arriving fresh from his obedience class there was mutual and immediate recognition - almost akin to old army comrades falling into each other's warm embrace after a lengthy leave of absence. The only things missing were sandbags and strong ale. Thereafter, following an obligatory short walk, the usual paperwork and inevitably, the fee: 'We accept all credit and debit cards Mr Long.'

Shortly, with bureaucracy satisfied, off we *all* set - each full of eager anticipation for our common futures.

The three hour car journey home bothered him not at all. We employed a newer version of Darcey's house on the car's back seat which he took to immediately. From within its comfortable confines he was expectant when we occasionally paused for traffic but settled down again quickly afterwards. At Orchard House he inspected both house and garden and promptly declared them fit and acceptable. So much so that his strange new surroundings quickly became familiar territory and from the safety of *his* garden he's already given our nice next-door neighbour grief for having the temerity to place rubbish in *her* bins!

Chapter Four

...and then we were three

Settling in was made all the easier due to my wife's shrewd foresight in retaining most of Sam and Elle's creature comforts. (*NB. This the woman who was not enamoured with the prospect of another dog in the house!*) Patch's corporate collar and identity disc were replaced with smart new individual versions and his food preferences and sleeping arrangements quickly established. All that then remained was the bad behaviour and lameness.

For all his energetic tail wagging enthusiasm at being home, it quickly became obvious why Patch alarmed and troubled his first adopters who rapidly despaired of him. Denied anything that he considered *his* property or due, he growled and snarled aggressively so we could quite understand why he'd been returned to the re-homing centre in disgrace ...but terriers can be like that. The Darlington team had briefed us about various distraction techniques they'd employed to divert him and with a system of careful consistency and taking no prisoners, he'd calmed down to mild rumblings within a few days. We quickly realised that, a typical terrier, he's a very quick and willing learner, especially if there are treats to be had but, like all his breed, stubbornness, the odd tantrum and mild insubordination are never far from the surface.

Although we'd been warned that Patch had experienced some lameness, at the time of writing he's been fine. All Parsons are naturally agile and he's no exception. With all the daintiness of an All Black's second row forward he barges about the house and garden with no sign of discomfort. So as to remonstrate with our nice neighbours he has, shades of the Guys, taken to destroying our decorative hedging in order to assist his passage to the boundary fence where he endeavours to intimidate them. Grief!

Thankfully they are owned by their own stroppy Jack Russell so are amused rather than annoyed by Patch's clumsy antics.

His first visit to our vets for his introductory MoT was more or less uneventful. Given his prior form we'd arranged an early morning first in-line appointment so as to avoid other patients and this scheme worked well. Naturally interested in the waiting room's ambience and *interesting* smells, he was calm and well behaved and even managed to remain so when weighed by the nurse on a large corner platform scale. So far, so good. Then the vet; by which time good manners were progressively giving way to excitement, mild outrage and the real danger of cranky bad temper to follow. Already informed about his background the vet was understanding and only mildly concerned when a grumpy growl was considered necessary - a mild Sledging, just to let the visiting side down.

Attempts at bullying the vet notwithstanding, Patch has been declared sound in wind and limb and because of the practice's new policy, his first appointment was free.

After a couple of days acclimatisation, a first walk. We'd been advised to use a muzzle as he'd been inclined to be snappy when meeting other dogs but training him to accept it had not been completed. Choosing a quiet time and a nearby lane known to be peaceful, my wife opted to use a Halti training lead because, according to Halti's advertising blurb: 'Where the nose goes - the dog goes' and anyway, we still hadn't *quite* persuaded Patch to accept his muzzle. Even with the best laid Cunning Plan a gentleman pedestrian and then a lady walker with her two dogs were unexpectedly encountered. For all the dire warnings of unpredictability, aggression and sheer bad temper, Patch demonstrated the very best of canine behaviour, sitting calmly when told and ignoring modest provocation. Further, it was apparent that he recognised many of the commands and signals we'd used to good effect with Darcey, Sam and Elle.

It was abundantly clear to us that, after Patch's earlier, clearly settled and well ordered lifestyle - and even with the very best of Dogs Trust care - major upheavals and turmoil with all their attendant uncertainties, had spawned grave anxiety, stress and confusion in him. Was it any surprise that he growled, snarled and snapped when challenged?

All in all he's gently ingratiating himself, clearly realizing that if he behaves, like us he's onto a good thing for the evening of his years. We are, as will be remembered, inveterate doggy folk.

Afterword

It's been three weeks since Patch came home. In that short period he's settled down to enjoying family life here as though he's been with us forever - even to the extent of eating, and patently enjoying the orchard's windfall apples. Our occasional visitors have observed how much he's calmed down and how well he's adjusted to life at Orchard House.

Just this morning my wife remarked how lucky it was for us that his first adopters sent him back. They'll never know what they've missed!

I wrote that afterword in late summer 2022. Some six months later readers might care to know that Patch has become a minor social media celebrity. Our on-line friends and relations are all keen to know about him and his adventures, so much so that in order to satisfy his eager audience I enquired about his past. Fortunately my Dogs Trust mole came up trumps with a mini biography:

Patch's narrative starts as a youngster when he arrived at a rescue centre having been handed in as a stray. He was quickly adopted by a family who cared for him for some eleven years until their declining health meant they could not give him all the care and attention he needed. With much regret they consigned him to Dogs Trust care.

'*...I think that they obviously loved him very much as they speak of him with a lot of affection and even mention him looking out of the window to guard the home and say that it's not in an aggressive way. They hope that he gets a loving home as he is a special dog.*'

I like to think we've come up to expectations.

Still on guard!

Some grateful acknowledgements

Any number of folk and organizations deserve our thanks. In no particular order:

Sea France and P&O Ferries, together with the Ports of Dover and Calais, merit a mention.

I am hugely grateful to the owners, managers and staff of the various B&Bs, Logis de France hotels, restaurants, pubs and of course, the cottages without whom none of this would have been possible. They have my unqualified gratitude.

You Know Who, the officer-in-charge and editor-in-chief played a captain's innings. She put up with much, provided encouragement and uncomplainingly ploughed through many drafts, correcting my inevitable mistakes in the later stages of our trip with Darcey with a blue finger rather than a red pencil. Although oft times sorely tempted - there being 'Nothing more dangerous than an officer (*in-charge*) with a map' - I won't be trading her in for a newer model anytime soon. Her tea and toast are exemplary, as all four of our dogs confirm.

Nikki Ellen of Crockshard Farm, who is one of the cast and who kindly read an early draft, told me that the Griffin's Head pub is actually 13th century. She went on to venture that her youngest daughter would most likely be mortified by my observations and concluded her welcome critique by revealing that the cat's name is Basil.

I have used the odd quote and at various points, Toad and Ratty from *The Wind in the Willows* seemed particularly appropriate as did Beth Norman Harris' evocative poetry.

Also I gratefully acknowledge the late great and sadly missed, Chairman Humph[3] of the BBC Radio 4's *I'm Sorry I Haven't a Clue* team and of course the man himself, for the Lionel Blair charades line. Something I simply could not resist. Anyway, whilst certainly not aspiring to her literary league, I'm Mrs Trellis of North Wales' greatest fan.

Whilst on matters literary, were it not for Peter Mayle's writing …and Henry's mum, another contented resident of Provence who we met in a castle in Fitou before all this started we might not have decided to explore the south of France at all.

The sub-aqua instructors at Mallorca's Petro Divers *Tauchschule* were hugely helpful when I was stung by jellyfish. (Medusa *in the local vernacular.*) I had to provide my own vinegar.

The Saab convertible and the Jeep Wrangler were huge successes. With the Wrangler I was much more relaxed on the ferries' car decks, in parking slots and various tight corners than I'd ever been before - and much less concerned when it was covered in mud and the inevitable dog hair. Frankly I'd never have managed the Camargue's tracks and byways in the Saab but that said, let me be clear. I don't for one moment decry posh cars - in reasonable conditions they are just as capable and

---

[3] Humphrey Lyttelton. (*1921 – 2008*) Jazz musician and broadcaster.

robust and probably a much more comfortable ride. It's just my innate caution and by now, well rehearsed, loathing of Dinkers and Dingers that shapes my opinion …and the Jeep's roof comes off. As time went by and our journey progressed, Wranglers seemed to be coming out of the woodwork - so clearly I'm not alone in my views.

We'd invested in some translation software before setting off and what a blessing it was. For a trifling sum we downloaded Systran's excellent programme, which came to the aid of the party on more than one occasion. If they could but arrange matters so as to enable voice recognition using a hand held device they'll rival Microsoft in no time at all.

I am hugely grateful to those Unfortunates who have taken the time and trouble to read and comment on the various drafts of these books. I can only hope they enjoyed the chuckle.

Thanks are also due to Cass Samways of the Parson Russell Terrier Club, Ciara Farrell of the Kennel Club who came to the aid of the party.

I am also indebted to a pair of literary professionals:

My editor Kitty Walker was tremendously influential in shaping and polishing the book.

Stuart Leasor decided the book was worth publishing and patiently shared his experience, enthusiasm, skill and good humour with a comrade-in-arms. He has my unreserved appreciation and thanks.

I'm conscious that our local Veterinary Surgeons played their part but hitherto I've failed to give them the credit they so richly deserve. My thanks go to all of the Pike Moor gang for their tender, thoroughly professional, always friendly and not quite costly, services.

Then there were Leigh Dog's Home and the Dogs Trust - what's to add?

Mea culpa

Finally, '...and thank goodness' did I hear? The many errors of fact, mistakes, false impressions, perversions, contradictions, and unadulterated nonsense are entirely my fault. Would that I could blame someone else. My cast of characters bear no relation to anyone living or dead.

Appendix

Treat Me Kindly

Treat me kindly my beloved friend, for no heart in all the world is more grateful for kindness than the loving heart of me.

Do not break my spirit with a stick, for though I might lick your hand between blows, your patience and understanding will more quickly teach me things you would have me learn.

Speak to me often; for your voice is the world's sweetest music as you must know by the fierce wagging of my tail when your steps fall upon my waiting ear.

Please take me inside when it is cold and wet, for I am a domesticated animal, no longer accustomed to bitter elements. I ask no greater glory than the privilege of sitting at your feet besides the hearth.

Keep my bowl filled with fresh water, for I cannot tell you when I suffer thirst.

Feed me clean food that I may stay well, to romp and play and do your bidding, to walk at your side and stand ready, willing and able to protect you with my life, should your life be in danger.

And, my friend, when I am very old, and I no longer enjoy good health, hearing and sight, do not make heroic efforts to keep me going. I am no longer having any fun. Please see that my trusting life is taken gently. I shall leave this earth knowing with the last breath I draw that my fate was always safest in your hands.

Beth Norman Harris 1968.

About the author

RB (*Rob*) Long grew up in the optimistic bright new world of the 60s when the shifting values and sinful ways, the Beatles, the mini skirts and the galloping hormones all contributed to him making a complete dog's dinner of his GCE O level exams.

Encouraged by his headmaster he joined the army straight from school and rose through the ranks before resigning to becoming an apprentice civilian some twenty-six years later. He joined a large national company as a corporate *consigliere* before being appointed its CEO. During this time he read for the degree he should have undertaken so much earlier. Later after successfully running two smaller concerns, he took early retirement.

A Parson Russell Terrier enthusiast, Francophile, wine buff and amateur historian, *The Best Deal* is his first book.

Printed in Great Britain
by Amazon

21901405R00142